PAUL JUHASZ

Fulfillment: Diary of a Warehouse Picker

FINE DOG
PRESS

First published by Fine Dog Press 2020

Copyright © 2020 by Paul Juhasz

First edition

ISBN: 978-1-7339795-7-3

This book was professionally typeset on Reedsy.
Find out more at reedsy.com

For P.J., and Emerson, for whom I endured.

And for Brian Mitchell, who made the enduring possible.

"An' they go nuts, an' you see 'em an' hear 'em, an' pretty soon you don' know if you're nuts or not. When they get to screamin' in the night sometimes you think it's you doin' the screamin'—an' sometimes it is."

— John Steinbeck, *The Grapes of Wrath*

Preface

In George Lucas's seminal sci-fi epic, *Star Wars*, Obi-Wan Kenobi stands on a rugged cliff on the desert planet Tatooine. Beside him is his soon-to-be Jedi apprentice, Luke Skywalker. Below them lies the port city of Mos Eisley. Kenobi turns to Skywalker, gestures toward the city below, and declares "You will never find a more wretched hive of scum and villainy."

Obi-Wan has clearly never worked in a warehouse distribution center.

I, unfortunately, have.

In May, 2013, the community college at which I was teaching accepted a grant from Wal-Mart, the terms of which mandated how I was to conduct my Freshman Composition class. Assignments, course content, and lesson plans were now determined by the terms of the grant, not by me. Unwilling to accept these conditions, I quit. After a fruitless three-month job search, I decided that some income was better than no income and began a seven-month stint as a night-shift picker at a major online vendor's warehouse distribution complex.

A "Fulfillment Center" is a massive building, stretching well over a standard city block. At either end are the Mods — each several football fields in area — consisting of three floors of rows of bins in which most of the products the company offers are stored. Throughout this expanse, pickers scurry about, ten to twelve hours per shift, incessantly collecting purchased items for shipments. Constant motion is a requirement. Shift expectations are twelve-hundred plus picks, which works out to a pick every thirty seconds. Each picker has a hand-held scanner that assigns a computer-generated pick path and counts down the time that same computer program has calculated is necessary to travel to and locate that pick. If you fail to hit this mark, the countdown on the scanner flashes red, the Process Assistant (P.A.) Managers are notified, and you are frequently called to account for your slow pace.

The standard minutiae of most Americans' work days are absent here. Reflexive acts, like going to the bathroom when you wish, talking to co-workers, or tying one's shoes, are risky. From management's perspective, these deviations from one's pick path are termed "Time Off Task" (T.O.T.) and will eventually lead to a "Come to Jesus" summons from whichever P.A. is on duty. Because the computer program that calculates rate cannot predict how items will pack in a tote or when carts need to be offloaded onto conveyor belts, pickers frequently hit T.O.T. for simply doing their jobs. Pickers who do not "make rate" — that is, achieve 100% efficiency — are soon fired.

The products not stored in either Mod are kept in a netherworld known by pickers as Palletland. Here one typically finds new release books and DVDs, bulk items, and products — like food processors or gallon jugs of peanut oil — too large for Mod bins. Generally, pickers struggle in Palletland; fewer items fit into totes and there are no conveyor belts to rush products up to the Pack department. When totes are full, pickers must push the oversized, harder-to-maneuver carts into the nearest section of the West Mod and offload there. Because of the nature of Palletland and its negative impact on rate, no picker is supposed to be assigned to Palletland for more than a quarter shift. This policy, however, is rarely honored.

At the end of a normal shift, pickers have walked, non-stop, *at least* fifteen to eighteen miles each night. Physically exhausted, they must then go through metal detectors and security pat-downs before they are excused to go home. Most block schedules are four or five consecutive days, so one's body rarely has time to heal from one shift before the next one begins. As the physical toll on the body escalates, rate suffers, and unemployment usually follows. One P.A. brazenly characterized the situation thusly: "There are so many people waiting to work here (this company typically pays slightly more than surrounding industries), we'll just use you guys up and when you're spent, we'll replace you."

The working conditions, as one would expect with managerial views such as this, have become somewhat notorious. In the summer of 2011, a local newspaper broke the story of a wave of heat stroke amongst the employees. With temperatures frequently topping 110 degrees in the warehouse, management refused to open loading bay doors to allow air to circulate. Instead, they contracted with a local ambulance company to have a line of vehicles parked outside, waiting to haul overcome workers to local hospitals. It was only after OSHA enforcement that air conditioners were installed.

And this was the world I had just decided to enter. When I made this decision, I had unknowingly entered a tightly secured world that was part *Blade Runner*, part *Lord of the Flies*, and part *Monty*

Python; a world of systemic exploitation, depersonalized cruelty, unimaginable bizarreness, and impossible people. While there, I kept a journal, either furtively scribbled in whenever I was far enough ahead of rate to be able to spare the time, or at home at the end of the shift. This journal is a testimony to the inconceivable weirdness that became my daily medium, to the casual exploitation of thousands of people, to the hidden cost of the instant gratification of consumer wish-fulfillment offered by a limitless virtual warehouse and free second-day shipping.

But mostly, since I quit a job where I was an overworked, fully exploited, dehumanized worker smothered by the incomprehensible dictates of an overreaching corporation, only to take a job where I was an overworked, fully exploited, dehumanized worker smothered by the incomprehensible dictates of an overreaching corporation, this journal is proof that, at the end of the day, I am not a very bright person.

I

The Diary

The Diary

Day 1:

I have, I fear, entered an odd, incongruent world.

This fact became apparent a few hours into the new employee orientation, when I (along with four dozen other new hires) was turned over to HR's head trainer, self-identified only as "The Sarge." A squat, grizzled, mid-60ish barrel with an iron-gray flat top, wearing a faded green T-shirt emblazoned with the order to "Kiss Me, I'm Irish," The Sarge reminded me of a Ralph Steadman sketch made flesh.

He began his presentation with a discussion of the company's zero-tolerance policy toward workplace violence. Any verified case of an associate threatening another associate, we were told, would result in immediate termination.

But as he informed us of this commitment to a violence-free workplace, he interrupted himself to tell two of our group chatting in the back that if they did not stop talking while he was talking, he would "smash your skulls together and have Maintenance dump your lifeless bodies in the Dumpster out back."

The Sarge is, I thought to myself, a funny man.

2nd entry:

The Sarge, as it turns out, is not a funny man. He is merely unintentionally ironic.

The second portion of his presentation featured a video meant to highlight the damaging impact of sexual harassment and racial discrimination in the workplace. When the video was over, The Sarge reinforced its message, emphatically asserting that there was a zero-tolerance sexual harassment and racial discrimination policy here.

The Sarge then called roll, assigning each of us to smaller training groups.

To Kevin Koswalski, he directed: "Kevin Kos-work-ski-in group-ski three-ski."

For Manuel, a middle-aged Hispanic man, The Sarge added: "Good, we now literally have some Manuel labor."

After assigning a young 20-something woman named Riann to Group Five, he unabashedly leered at her ass as she passed, and while the cacophony of conveyor belts, forklifts, and other assorted automated rumblings make it difficult to say with any certainty, I am pretty sure I heard him make a yummy sound.

After he worked through about two dozen names, he announced, "And yet another Hispanic. Did you all ride in together?"

To my surprise, he then called my name, and the following conversation ensued:

Me: "Um, I'm not Hispanic."

The Sarge: "Last name's Juhasz, right?"

Me: "Yes, but it's not Hispanic."

The Sarge: "Well, Ju-haz, 'yu has' a funny last name. Sounds Hispanic."

Me: "It's Hungarian."

4

The Sarge: "Oh, a Limey, huh? Group Three."

I think I may have made a mistake coming here. I think if I was a smart man, I would run away from here as fast as I can. I think if I was a smart man, I'd never come back.

Day 2:

I am not a smart man.

Turns out I don't actually work for The Company; I work for a temp agency whose only client is The Company.

The majority of the employees here in fact are temp workers. This allows The Company to avoid paying benefits to a large portion of its workforce and insulates them from unemployment and workers' comp claims. It's a fairly ingenious arrangement that certainly would win the approval of 19th-century robber barons.

Of course, this is not how the partnership was presented to us. During orientation, our trainer explained it thusly:

"The Company is like a big shark, and you temp workers are like remoras."

I think she was trying to be helpful.

I also fear I may have made a mistake coming here.

Day 3:

There is a noticeable undercurrent of rage among these people.

In the cafeteria during lunch break, I witnessed a disturbing exchange between an older African American male and a half-dozen 20-somethings.

As they sat under a television re-broadcasting the Home

Run Derby, the older man was loudly mocking the Mets' third baseman, David Wright. With every out, the man would gleefully shout, "David Wright's an All-Star, huh?" and immediately glance over at the young men, two of whom were wearing Mets caps.

One of the Mets fans made the mistake of muttering a response, and the older man pounced.

Grabbing him by the shirt collar, he screamed, "Open your mouth again and I will take a blow torch to your face!"

While I was certainly impressed with the specificity and the creativity of the threat, what fascinated me most was that The Sarge, who placidly sat at a nearby table, apparently did not consider this a violation of the zero-tolerance workplace violence policy.

It's almost certain I made a mistake coming here.

Day 4:

Tonight was my first foray into the Mods. My first pick was a yodeling pickle.

WTF?

Day 5:

I find myself in a strange land.

For ten hours, I walk a grid of interminable aisles, looking for bras with wine pouch inserts and yodeling pickles, all the while holding back tears because I live in a world where bras with wine pouch inserts and yodeling pickles exist and where people buy them.

6

It occurs to me that, as a species, we may be doomed.

Day 6:

My co-workers are a decidedly odd, almost cartoonish, bunch. For example, there is a 6'6" Jamaican who wears a faded and dirty tuxedo jacket with tails and a stovepipe hat for every shift and mumbles to himself continuously.

There is also an old lady who carries around a bag of Dum-Dum lollipops and hands you one whenever you pass her. But the thing is, she has a very poor memory and gives you one every time she sees you. Depending on your pick path, you can end the shift with two dozen of these things.

There's also someone labeled "The Masturbator." He's earned this name because each night precisely at 11:40, 2:30, and again at 4:15, he locks himself in the single stall bathroom at the back of the West Mod and jerks off.

But perhaps the oddest of the bunch is Matt. There are about eight hundred employees here each shift. Matt is so exhaustingly annoying that he is on speaking terms with only about thirteen of them.

I, apparently, and through no volition of my own, am one of the thirteen.

I think thirteen is a very unlucky number.

This is what a sample conversation with Matt is like:

Matt: "Do you like the G.I. Joe movies?"

Me: "Haven't seen them."

Matt: "Which one is your favorite?"

Me: "Um, I haven't seen any of them?"

Matt: "Did you see the latest one?"

Me: "Is this thing on? No. I haven't."

Matt: "I can *not* believe they killed off Duke! Why would they do that?"

I pondered politely reminding him that I just said I didn't see the movie. Instead, because I'm a dumbass, I respond:

"I don't know. Maybe the writers thought they had exhausted the depth of the character and there was really nowhere else to go with him."

(awkward silence)

Matt: "Huh?"

I sigh, then give Matt the reply I know he wants: "Man, COBRA is just fucking evil!"

Matt shakes his head knowingly. "I know, man. I know."

(fist bump)

Day 7:

I'm not too sure about my manager, Mike. A lanky, weasel-faced man in his mid-40s sporting a ghost-white flattop and a perpetual three-day stubble, Mike's hobby seems to be breaking our balls.

Yesterday, when our lunch was pushed back an hour and a half, I heard him say to the lollipop lady, for whom this delay seemed to represent a hardship, that "if I had my way, none of you would eat until all the orders were out the door."

Tonight, he announced we would be working six days this week due to a volume backload.

"Only," he added, "because it's against the law to work you seven."

8

It occurs to me that Mike may be a dick.

Day 8:

Exhausted and sore, I wasn't really paying attention when I sat down at the cafeteria table during break, so it wasn't until he asked the question that I realized I was sitting next to the Angry Man from last week's Home Run Derby disagreement.

Angry Man: "Do you know what that motherfucker just said to me?"

I didn't even know who the motherfucker in question was, so I had very little chance of getting this question right.

Me: "Um, that you're wearing his jacket?"

Angry Man: "Get the fuck out of here!"

I furtively scanned his hands and then his pockets, looking for any sign of a blowtorch.

"I have no idea," I tried again.

Angry Man: "He said Terrell Owens is not a Hall of Fame receiver. Terrell Fucking Owens! Can you believe that shit?"

Me: "Um, no way man."

Angry Man's silence seemed to indicate more was expected from me, so I added: "That motherfucker's crazy."

Angry Man: "Damn straight!"

He then got up and left.

As I sat at the table in silence, I realized that this was my first close interaction with a psychopath.

I didn't really like it.

Day 9:

Tonight's shift raised two very important questions:

"What kind of party is the soon-to-be-owner of a 64 oz bottle of Passion Lube planning?"

And:

"Can I come?"

Day 10:

America is now a place where we sell pre-sharpened pencils.

I respectfully suggest that we may be coddling our children too much.

Day 11:

This is a bizarre, illogical place.

For example, in section D on the third floor of the east Mod, there is a locked cage, extending two dozen rows or so, where high-end items such as iPods and iPhones are stored.

This makes sense.

Only employees who have worked here for a lengthy period of time and have a spotless discipline record are given access to this cage.

This also makes sense.

But the cage is not situated at the back of the section (which would make sense) or even at the front (which would also make sense) but is placed dead-smack in the middle of the section. This means all pickers working in this section, when their pick path moves them from rows before the cage to rows behind the cage must divert into Section C — a detour that our scanners do not account for, resulting in lost time and, ultimately, poor rate numbers, and T.O.T. talks.

I may have made a mistake coming here.

Day 12:

Tonight, a story made the rounds about a picker who was diagnosed with plantar fasciitis. Yesterday, he came to work with a note from his doctor limiting him to light duty only.

Mike had him sweep the factory floor for 10 hours.

I'm reasonably certain Mike is a dick.

Day 13:

There are two types of totes here: green ones and yellow ones. Each has specific rules governing their use. For example, yellow totes can be stacked twelve high, while the greens can be stacked fifteen high.

Each has a specific place in the Mods where they are stored. And those places are marked with signage.

Where the green totes go, there are green signs reading "Stack Green Totes Here." I find this sign quite efficient, even a touch elegant, in its straightforward simplicity.

Where the yellow totes go is also marked with signage, reading "Stack Yellow Totes Here."

But this sign is *not* yellow; this sign is also green.

There lurks an evil presence in this place. It feeds and grows strong on my confusion.

Day 14:

When I originally posted the previous entry on Facebook, a friend asked me the following question: "Hey Paul, what's a tote?"

My response: "A tote is a plastic box in which pickers place our picks. It should not be confused with a toke, which is frequently one over the line, Sweet Jesus."

Day 15:

The rabbit hole runs deeper than I thought.

Not only is the person tasked with teaching employees about the policies designed to promote a safe and respectful workplace a racist letch with anger management issues, but it has been brought to my attention that The Sarge has never been in the military, or on a police force, or a part of any organization that bandies about terms such as "rank" and "sergeant." He just declared one day that he was now a sergeant, and in this ridiculous world, a sergeant he became.

But I take some comfort in this latest evidence of an insane world.

As I drove home this morning, I decided a promotion was in order.

Starting tomorrow, I am the Burgermeister.

Day 16:

I told Mike I had some serious reservations about a small order I was picking.

Mike: "What's the problem?"

Me: "The order is just four items, Mike. Rope, Duck Tape, a jar of KY jelly, and a filet knife."

Mike: "So?"

Me: "You don't find this disturbing?"

Mike: "Not if his credit card clears."

I'm almost positive Mike is a dick.

Day 17:

During tonight's shift, I got to pick three dildoes and six bottles of anal lube.

Stay classy, America, stay classy.

Day 18:

Despite Mike's cavalier attitude a few days ago *vis-à-vis* the rape kit, I am of the opinion that I should be culturally deputized to veto picks.

If someone is buying a Yodeling Pickle, they really need to be protected from themselves.

Day 19:

I have quickly learned to dread pick paths that take me to first floor sections E and F.

It is the home of oversized products, where only one or two items fill a tote, and so you spend the shift rushing to the conveyor belts every two or three picks. If you listen closely, you can hear you rate numbers plummet.

It is a gloomy place, with less lighting than the other sections and, relatively speaking, it is quite deserted. On an average stay, you may only encounter three or four other pickers.

And if one of them is Matt, you're fucked.

It is also the preferred haunt of the janitor.

Given the size of this factory, there must be a several-person custodial staff, but I have only seen one janitor, and only in first floor sections E and F.

Tonight, I was speeding down the main corridor separating the two sections, desperately trying to get from aisle 123 to aisle 3 before my scanner's countdown ended when I saw him pushing his cart towards me, stopping at every trash can to see if it needed emptying.

I had already noticed that everyone ignores this janitor, and when I met his gaze, his cold, dead blue eyes not looking at, but through, me, I understood why.

But my grandfather always told me that a stranger is just a friend you haven't met yet, and so I determined to engage this fellow human being, no matter how creepy he was.

Me: "Hello."

The Janitor: "I'm the janitor."

Me: "Um, yes. I know. How are you tonight?"

The Janitor: "I'm the janitor."

Me: "Ok. Um, well, I need to get going. You have a great night."

The Janitor: "I'm the janitor."

My grandfather is a senile old man.

I need to stop listening to what he says.

Day 20:

These first few weeks have been a bit taxing, both physically, as I adjust to the rigors of walking eighteen miles a night without stop, four nights in a row, and mentally, as I struggle against dysfunctional policies and a kaleidoscope of freaks and weirdos I must now, through very modest fault of my own, call co-workers.

One of few palliatives so far is Wendell. Wendell is the place's wily old veteran. Meeting me in the Mod last night, he approached and hailed me with a "You're new here." We chatted a bit, each offering our "how'd you get here?" story — a ritualized exchange for the newly *simpatico*.

I only partially followed his tale, because I kept getting struck by just how much his wizened, wrinkled face and bushy, wheat-and-grey-colored mustache called to mind The Lorax. Since it was late, and mental fatigue had set in, it was all I could do not to ask him how the Brown Bar-Ba-Loots were doing.

At the end of the chat, though, he gave me some advice, the first of much to come:

"Don't kill yourself here. We got pickers so full of the shit management is spewing, that they bust themselves to get a rate of 180%, 200%. And they act all proud. Like they just did something for themselves. But here's the thing: Management doesn't give a fuck about them, or you, or me. They want to squeeze every last ounce of energy you have, and when you have nothing left to give, they'll fire your ass and replace it."

With that, and a somewhat incongruous avuncular pat on the shoulder, he resumed his pick path and left me to resume mine.

As far as speeches go, this was not exactly "I am the Lorax and I speak for the trees."

"What an odd and melodramatic man," I thought to myself.

Day 21:

Wendell is *not* a melodramatic man.

The word on the floor is the guy with plantar fasciitis who Mike had sweeping the factory as "light duty" is now unemployed.

He was fired because "he could no longer physically perform the duties for which he was hired."

I may have made a mistake coming here.

Day 22:

There's a guy here with Tourette's.

The managers treat him like a mascot, always picking him out to lead stretches during standup.

I must admit it is a bit distracting to hear him insert an "asshole" or a "douche bag" into his ten counts.

His impulsive cursing is more jarring in the Mods, though.

Engulfed within the solitariness of one's pick path, hearing a booming cry of "Shit!" or "Poop, poopy, poopness!" or turning into an aisle and having him suddenly yell "Fuckface" at you before he moves on, is just a bit disconcerting.

At the same time, there is an unmistakable aptness to it that is, at the very least, consistent with this setting.

Day 23:

Can there really be such a thing as *The Essential Michael Bolton*?

Day 24:

Another conversation with Matt:

He approaches, as if continuing an earlier conversation:

Matt: "So, like I was saying, my cousin turns twenty today. Yeah, he's a fourth generation American. I'm a third generation, so he's a fourth."

Me: "That would be true only if you were your cousin's father" (which, I reflect, is a possibility I should not be so quick to dismiss).

Matt (oblivious to the interruption): "My mom is second generation and my grandmother, well, she came over here from Ireland. Or was it Slovakia? I can never remember which one it is."

Me: "That's understandable. I suppose those two countries get mixed up all the time."

Matt: "Yeah, so, like I was saying. She came over in 1912, so she's a first generation . . ."

Me: "That's not how it works. If she came over, she wasn't born here. So she's not a first generation American. She's a last generation Irishslovakian. Your mother is a first generation, you're a second, and who the hell knows what's up with your cousin."

Matt is silent a moment, then: "Yeah, that's what I was saying. My grandmother would be a first generation, since she came over in 1912 . . ."

Me (turning to run away): "I think I hear the fire alarm."

Day 25:

I would have been just fine never learning that I live in a world where one can buy a bacon wallet.

Day 26:

For our comfort, the Company has provided the break area at the East Mod with a TV, three vending machines (one with soda, one with coffee, and one with snacks), and, inexplicably, a microwave.

Since facility policy prohibits us from bringing food from home onto the factory floor, one wonders what management thinks employees could be interested in microwaving.

Do Funyuns, perhaps, taste better heated?

2nd entry:

Funyuns do *not* taste better when heated.

Day 27:

I had been moving full totes of Ramen noodles from Palletland to a conveyor belt for almost six hours. Looking at my scanner, I noted it was 11:58. Knowing that if I went back to the Ramen pallet, made the pick, and returned to the belt, I'd be burning up my lunch break, I docked my cart.

"Should we still pay you for those two minutes?"

Turning, I saw Mike glaring at me from behind his desk.

"Excuse me?" I asked.

"I was just wondering, since you docked two minutes early, if you thought we should pay you for those two minutes?"

"Mike, I've been in Palletland all night. No one's supposed to work there two straight quarters, but I didn't complain. And if I make my next pick, I won't get my full break. You know, the one mandated by law?"

A beat or two of silence.

"So, you *don't* want to get paid for those two minutes, then?"

"You're really gonna ride my ass about this?" I asked incredulously.

"No," Mike replied. "I'm not going to ride your ass. I'm going to tell Payroll to deduct two minutes from your paycheck this week."

With that, Mike pivoted and walked away.

Looking at my scanner, I saw I would be late for lunch anyway.

This place sucks.

And Mike is *definitely* a dick.

Quite possibly a big one.

Like, massive.

Day 28:

Had a fascinating discussion with some of my fellow pickers tonight. Turns out Mike is not my manager. Our boss is the shift supervisor, Will, who spends the vast majority of each shift either in the bathroom or in the cafeteria. I think he is afraid of us.

Mike is a P.A. (Process Assistant).

Beyond telling us when we are not making rate, Mike has no actual supervisory authority over us.

I find this interesting.

2nd entry:

Mike was not in a good mood this evening. It seems that someone left a jar of Vaseline on his desk, with a hastily-scribbled note on it that read:

"For Process Assistance"

I think he suspects I had something to do with it.

Day 29:

Mike was in a *really* bad mood tonight. He read us the riot act, bandying about phrases like "know your place" and "respect for leadership." As Fascist rants go, it would have been quite impressive if his dour earnestness didn't make it seem so melodramatic and just a little bit ridiculous.

Apparently, what set him off was a poster board sign someone had taped to the P.A. desk, which read:

Mike's Male Enhancement Fund:

Because shouldn't a big dick *have* a big dick?

What I thought most odd was that in the donation jar affixed above the sign was $0.43, or exactly what my salary for two minutes of work would be.

I walked into the Mod to start my shift struck by this amazing coincidence.

Day 30:

Tonight, I picked an AC/DC tester.

Curious, I tried it on myself.

Turns out I'm Back in Black.

Day 31:

I mentioned to Mike that walking the standard 15-18 miles per night encased in the ejaculation of a consumer world gone mad like a human mosquito trapped in amber would suck slightly less if we could listen to some music on an iPod or something. He replied that we can't, because The Company sells iPods and there would be no way for security to know if the ones we had were truly ours or were stolen from the warehouse.

I thought about this for a moment, then mentioned that The Company also sells pants, and so, to make life more bearable for security, I would volunteer to stop wearing any from now on.

He didn't say anything. He just looked at me for a moment or two, then turned and walked away.

I don't think he likes me very much.

Day 32:

My mother always used to tell me that there's one weirdo on every bus. I can never find him.

Here, though, there is no such problem. I can throw a rock (of course, I would never bring a rock into the Mods, for the Company may sell rocks and I don't want to vex security) and hit any one of a large number of assorted oddballs, ne'er-do-wells and impossibly strange people.

I met the latest member of this menagerie tonight.

I don't know his name. He's in his early twenties. And he is tall. Very tall. 6'4"ish at the very least. He has a long face and unnaturally long arms that hang down below his knees, giving him a somewhat simian look. He courses through the Mods with an odd, bouncing stride, almost genuflecting with each step.

I nearly collided with him as I turned out of an aisle, pulling up short as he raced down toward the other end of the Mod.

"My bad," I apologized.

He showed no sign of having heard me, nor of noting my presence. His gaze remained transfixed ahead of him as he raced down, turning at last into a distant aisle.

I found the experience unsettling.

I think, based on his physical appearance, his gait, and the aura of creepiness surrounding him, I shall call him Lurch.

Day 33:

I walked past a gender prediction kit.

I assume the box contains a magnifying glass and the following instructions:

1)Look for a penis
2)Repeat if necessary

Day 34:

During stand-up, Mike rambled on about the importance of damaging out picks if there is a problem. Apparently, it's kind of a big deal when a customer gets broken crap. Seems they tend not to be happy. Whatever.

He goes on and on about this and closes with the invitation that "if you can't determine if something is broken, bring it to me and I'll help you."

I decide to take him up on this later in the shift, bringing over a Lego set and saying "I think something's broken in here."

I shake the box, so he can hear all the pieces rattling about. "See?"

He rubs his face with both hands and says "Paul, get back to work."

I don't think he likes me very much.

2nd entry:

Undaunted by my earlier failure, I brought Mike another broken item, this time a Stanley stud finder.

Mike looked over the item, "Looks fine to me. What's wrong with it?"

I took the stud finder from him and placed it on my chest. "See? Nothing happens. It must be broken."

Day 35:

Today I picked a tube of 100% Pure Moroccan Oil.

It shouldn't be legal to do that to Moroccans.

Day 36:

As I steered my cart into aisle B 34, I ran into Lurch.

"Hey, what's up?" I greeted him.

No response.

Not even a head nod.

He silently and impassively walked towards his next pick.

I think maybe he's deaf.

When I ran into Matt later, I found myself envying Lurch.

Day 37:

For the second time in as many days, I nearly collided with Lurch's cart as I turned out of an aisle.

For the second time in as many days, I offered up a "My bad"

(It really wasn't. But I was taught to be polite).

For the second time in as many days, there was zero recognition from Lurch that I had spoken or that I even existed.

I think he may be a cyborg.

Day 38:

I've been aware of — and more than a bit perplexed by — the monstrously-tall Jamaican picker dressed each shift in a dirty tuxedo jacket and stovepipe hat who spends the entirety of each shift muttering to himself. But it was not until tonight that my pick path brought me close enough to make out what this hulking six and half foot tall (seven when you consider the hat) man spends ten hours a day, four days a week, repeating, in his thickly-accented English:

"Four score and seven years ago."

My life, it is now clear, has become a David Lynch movie.

That, or I got a hold of some bad acid and Woodstok Farley is not here to talk me through this trip.

Day 39:

Why does *The Never-Ending Story* have a running time of 102 minutes?

Day 40:

It occurs to me that I not only see the janitor solely in sections E and F, but that when I do, he is always pushing his custodial cart up the main corridor; never anywhere else.

It's like he's a figure from Greek myth, banished to Tartarus and condemned to forever walk this corridor, perpetually emptying ceaselessly filling trash cans.

This is the most compelling evidence I've found that I am in hell.

Day 41:

What bothers me about most of the people I work with is that they actually exist, even when that existence is by any standard preposterous.

For example: Brad.

Brad is a walking caricature. I struggle daily to believe he's real and not some atavistic cliché my mind, in an attempt to process the general absurdity of this place, has projected outward. He is literally the stereotypical dirty old man. Mid-60s, pear-shaped body, a pock-marked face topped by a dirty grey crew cut. When he smiles, he reveals he has at least six or seven teeth (so he's got *that* going for him, which is nice). If he's not a registered sex offender, he ought to be.

And he behaves in a way that is simply impossible. "Perverted" doesn't even begin to cover it. He's a libido gone mad.

At times, I suspect he is not human, is in fact a satyr.

He'll complain during a break, to no one in particular, that the selection of pocket pussies sold here is disappointing, explaining he "likes 'em to have big bushes."

FULFILLMENT: DIARY OF A WAREHOUSE PICKER

Who the fuck does this?

One of the other things he likes to do is assail any female co-worker unfortunate enough to be near him with a constant barrage of dirty jokes, each one more offensively inappropriate than the last.

The other night he "treated" Mable (the lollipop lady) to a routine of such staggering crudity that left everyone in the break area speechless.

I sometimes wonder how HR hasn't canned this guy yet, then I walk by HR and see The Sarge. And then I say to myself: "Oh yeah."

This place sucks.

Day 42:

As the weeks go by and my feet get heavier, my thoughts duller, and my faith in the inherent dignity of each human life fades, Wendell has been there, offering sage advice at each turn.

He has taught me to grab the last item to pick before break and wait until I get to the conveyor belt before scanning it.

"That way, Mike won't get on your ass for making a pick 2-3 minutes before break and then stopping."

He has taught me to use three totes when picking in the E and F sections, even though this is a direct violation of "safety standards."

"Not even Mike scouts those sections. They're too far away from the P.A. desk."

And he has taught me to arbitrarily scan any bin every two minutes or so when I'm off task.

"Computers at the P.A. desk register the scan, but not where it is or if it's the right bin. It just records you as working, which resets the T.O.T. clock."

But he has not yet taught me how to avoid Matt, or a way to kill Mike and hide the body.

I find his teachings of limited value.

Day 43:

"Crunch Lovers."

I discovered this most odd pairing of words tonight on a box of crackers.

I have heard of "chocolate lovers," "spicy lovers," and "cheese lovers."

Thanks to Pizza Hut (and that is about the *only* time in my life I will utter that phrase), I have been introduced to the concept of "Meat Lovers" and "Veggie Lovers."

But this was "Crunch Lovers."

As in: Lovers of Crunch.

This means there is a significant enough snack-eating demographic who base their enjoyment of food on it being dry enough, bite-resistant enough, and loud enough to be disruptive to other near-by eaters.

First, I reacted to this information with wonder: "Who are these people for whom normal crackers are insufficient to satisfy their need for crunch?"

Then, I was concerned: "I sure hope there are none of these people in the theater next time I go see a movie."

Next, indignation: "Great, move over, Vegans! There's another militant group of needy, self-righteous eaters in town."

But finally, blissful acceptance of the diversity of the world:

"A group of people designed by Nature to enjoy my mother's cookies — dry, hard, pseudo-edible disks that they are."

So tonight, I celebrate you, "Crunch Lovers."

Louie Armstrong was right. It *is* a beautiful world. A beautiful world indeed.

Day 44:

Today Mike informed me I was selected to be converted.

I replied, "Hey! Slow down, Torquemada! I am quite content with my faith."

He indicated that he meant I was to be converted from a temp worker to an official employee of The Company.

"Is there a ceremony?" I asked.

"No," he tersely replied.

Trying hard to hide my disappointment, I asked Mike if he would be willing to wear a big, funny hat and chant in a dead language anyway.

He just turned and walked away.

I don't think he likes me very much.

Day 45:

I passed Lurch again this evening. Determined to be acknowledged, I asked if he planned to sign up for voluntary OT.

No reaction of any kind.

Maybe he's a ghost.

Day 46:

I just read on the label of a *men's* multi-vitamin bottle that I should consult with a doctor before taking if I am pregnant or nursing a baby.

Tears of rage blinded me the rest of the shift.

Day 47:

Since the conversion, I have noticed a change in the way I am treated by my fellow workers.

There is a distinct caste system in this place. Official employees are a lot like the Star-Bellied Sneetches; the *zeitgeist* holds that the official Company blue ID badge instills status and prestige, allowing Company workers to look down on the temps (who have no such badge upon thars).

While I am grateful and touched that they have now accepted me into their tribe and treat me like one of their own, I am determined to maintain a relationship similar to the ones cultivated by Jane Goodall and Dian Fossey before me.

I shall be among them, but not of them .

Day 48:

My fellow Star-Bellied Sneetches are an easily-confused lot, if one can draw any conclusions from the employee handbook.

Do I really need color-coded water bottles for each day of the week?

Our employee handbook insists this helps you stay organized and keep track of your schedule, which I guess may be true.

But so does paying attention.

Day 49:

I just passed Brad.

He was holding a DVD of a film creatively titled *Big Titty MILFs* #22. As I was walking by, he pointed at the accomplished actress on the cover, sighed longingly, and said "Reminds me of mother."

I have no words.

Truly none.

Except that this place sucks.

Day 50:

I was already thoroughly depressed even before I entered aisle A19, for I knew once I did, I would be picking a Fun Fin—a shark fin hat, "suitable for daily dry land use."

Which of course meant I shared the world with at least one person who woke up today and felt the one thing lacking in his or her life was the ability to wear a shark fin on their fucking head.

But shortly after I entered the aisle, Lurch entered from the other side.

I tried to engage him with some traditional intra-picker banality: "We just might make it to lunch break."

No response from Lurch.

He just made his pick, pushed his cart past me, his eyes never veering from their locked, straight-ahead stare, turned the corner and was gone.

Me? I found myself suddenly questioning a previously-unassailable belief in my own existence.

Until Matt turned the corner and explained to me in interminable detail why he likes kangaroos.

Then I knew I did indeed exist.

And that that existence was Hellish.

I hate this place.

Day 51:

Today, I was in line at Human Resources to complete some conversion paperwork when the girl in front of me turns, apparently notices that I have a tattoo on my arm, puts that together with my flat-top, and, inexplicably, my Old Navy t-shirt and says "Thank you for your service."

I didn't have the heart to tell her that I never worked there.

2nd entry:

Behind the HR counter was The Sarge. When I explained what I needed, he grabbed a roster of the new conversions and asked "Name?"

"The Colonel," I replied ('Burgermeister' had a shelf-life of about a week; everyone here assumed I had a second job in the fast food industry.)

"Huh?"

Recognizing my error (for there must, I thought, be several Colonels on the roster), I offered up my full title: "The Colonel of Doom."

"Stop shitting me! What's your real name?"

Disappointed (for I was of the mind that if anyone could appreciate the arbitrary assumption of a non-existent rank, it would be The Sarge) I gave my actual name.

"What is that, Mexican?" he asked.

"No, it's *still* not Hispanic."

"Hm, Juhasz? Sounds Mexican to me."

"Well, it's not."

He fixed me with a probing glare for a beat or two. "You sure?"

(sigh) "Reasonably."

"Sure sounds Mexican to me."

I hate this place.

Day 52:

I generally adopt a policy of avoiding dialog with crazy people whenever possible. It is a sound rule, and, except for one late-night drunken call to Charlie Sheen to demand he return the Molly Hatchet cassette he borrowed from me after we met at a sweat lodge ceremony in New Mexico, it's one I have not deviated from.

Until tonight.

I once again ran into the hat and tails wearing Jamaican, whom I've named Stovepipe Lincoln. After a few rotations of "Four score and seven years ago," curiosity trumped common sense and before I could remind myself of that solid and well-grounded rule, I asked him, "Why do you keep saying that?"

Stovepipe turned to me and flashed a big, comforting grin, as if he had been eagerly waiting for someone to ask him this, and replied:

"I love your Mr. Lincoln."

His grin then flattened into a tight-lipped glare.

"He keeps me free from de white people," he added.

He then turned and resumed both his pick path and his chant.

It is time I face a very unpleasant truth:

This place scares the hell out of me.

Day 53:

Since I'm a good father, I am trying to provide my sons with an expansive collection of action figures from the comic book worlds (both DC and Marvel) I loved as a kid.

So you can imagine my excitement when I saw in a bin adjacent to my pick an Invisible Woman (of the Fantastic Four) action figure.

And you can imagine my disappointment when I turned the packaging over to discover the box was empty.

Day 54:

I decided tonight to wear the new t-shirt that my mother got for me in Morocco. It's from Rick's Café, of *Casablanca* fame, and on the back it reads "The Legend continues."

On the way to the lunchroom during break, a co-worker reads the back out loud, slaps me on the shoulder and says, "I love that movie."

I replied, "Yeah, it is a great one. My mother just went to Morocco on vacation and when she asked what she could get me, I said 'go to Rick's and get me a t-shirt...'"

He looked quite puzzled, and despite knowing the depression that would follow, I offered the observation that "I think we may be talking about different movies."

He replied, "I was talking about *Kung Fu: The Legend Continues*." He then strikes what I assume was intended as an authentic kung-fu pose.

This place sucks.

Day 55:

Apparently, consistently hitting rate is not good enough here. Mike informed me that he would "prefer" I push past 100% and strive for a higher rate number.

After confirming that he did in fact understand the meaning of "per cent," I clarified that he was asking me to do more than what was required.

"Yes. That's the synergy we like to see out of our pickers."

"And I assume my paycheck would then also be more than is required?"

"Um, no. No, your paycheck would be the same."

"So, you want me to do more work for the same pay?"

"That's what we'd like to see."

"Yes, I bet you would."

I then returned to the Mod to resume my carefully calibrated 100% rate pace.

2nd entry:

Knowing Mike hates shipping damaged product, I brought him a bag of assorted Hershey's Candy.

"Something's wrong with this," I told him.

"I see that. The bag is opened. Nice catch, Paul."

"No, *I* opened the bag. That's not the problem."

"What is, then?"

"Well, there's only 100 pieces in there."

"That's because there's supposed to be 100 pieces," he explained, pointing to the label on the bag that read "100 Pieces."

"And why did you open the bag to count?" he added.

"Well, I thought the customer would prefer it had 106 pieces. I'm betting that's the synergy they'd like to see out of their bags of candy."

Mike stared silently at me for a minute, then told me to get back to work.

I don't think he appreciates my commitment to customer satisfaction.

I also think he doesn't like me very much.

Day 56:

Tonight, my pick path intersected Lurch's again.

Desperate for some type of recognition, I asked "Hey, do you know what time it is?"

Nothing.

I tried again.

"Hey, man. Your shoes are untied."

Still nothing.

Overcome with frustration, I tried one more time.

"Hey, later on, I'm going to shit in your hair."

Nothing.

I am forced to admit that Lurch may be the creation of a mind whose sanity is crumbling.

Day 57:

This place is not only ridiculous; it is also dangerous and potentially lethal.

And tonight, my time was almost up.

As I grabbed an item from a top bin, one, then two pairs of women's pajamas fell on my head. My reflexes momentarily dulled by the successive blows, I was unable to avoid the avalanche of dozens more pajamas. Soon, I was prone on the floor, buried in an ever-growing pile of satin.

My final thoughts before the darkness took me were "No, Dear Lord! Not like this. It can't end like this. Not like Grandpa."

Day 58:

Today's generation has it far too easy. They expect instant gratification and refuse to work or earn what they want.

You can now buy an ankle monitor to wear as an accessory, to show (one supposes) what a bad-ass you are.

When I was growing up, if you wanted an ankle monitor, you had to earn it by knocking over a convenience store.

I weep for the future.

Day 59:

During stand-up, Mike mentioned that on a normal shift, we have more than seven-hundred people working in the warehouse.

"We're like a small town," he explained.

After stand-up, I approached Mike's desk.

"What do you want, Paul?"

"Can I be the mayor?"

"What?"

"The mayor. You said we're like a small town. I'd like to be mayor."

Rubbing his face with his hands, he responded, "No, Paul, you can't be mayor. Now get back—"

"Councilman?"

"No."

"Alderman?"

"No!"

"First Selectman?"

"No!"

"Can I at least have epaulettes?"

"What the fuck are epaulettes?"

"Those shoulder board thingees important people wear?"

"No!"

"An important-looking hat?"

"No! Just get back to work!"

I looked back at his desk before I entered the Mod.

He had his head in his hands.

I don't think he likes me very much.

Day 60:

I blasted the radio on the commute tonight, hoping to get a good song in my head or be inspired by some positive message.

Instead, I was forced to confront just how off I've been about the lyrics to "Aqualung."

Day 61:

Yet another unsolicited conversation with Matt.

Matt: "Yeah, I got about 32 friends on Facebook now. I'm pretty popular."

Me: "32?! Wow, um, that's a lot."

Matt: "Yeah. It is. I got one the other day from Poland. He has the same last name as I do. We must be related."

I consider pointing out that I was under the impression that Ireland and/or Slovakia was the land of his ancestors.

I also consider saying nothing and moving on to my next pick.

Instead, because I am not very smart, I reply: "Poland? Wow, that's far away."

Matt: "Yeah. Much farther than New Jersey. It's kinda tough, though, when he writes me. I have no idea what he's saying. It's like he's talking Greek."

Talking to Matt makes my brain hurt. I promise myself I'm going to stop doing it.

Day 62:

The Darwin Awards annually celebrate individuals who have contributed to the human gene pool by removing themselves from it.

For example, in 2000, a young Houston man reportedly decided to play Russian Roulette. The problem was, his gun was not a revolver (which of course lends a titillating element of chance to the game), but a semi-automatic. For his lethal act of dumbassery, he was a Darwin Award winner.

It is merely a matter of time before someone here does something Darwin worthy.

Tonight, I may have met the leading candidate.

I was on the third floor when I heard a cry of "Gah!" immediately followed by a series of metal-, plastic-, wood-, and glass-on-metal crashes.

I recalled that during orientation, one of the trainers noted that short pickers frequently use the bottom two shelves as steps to reach the top shelf. Fearing that the noises I heard where the result of an aisle crashing down upon someone rash enough to do this, I rushed to the source.

Staring vacantly down the stairwell leading down to the 2nd level stood a new picker (Jake, as per his [non-blue] badge). At the bottom of the stairs lay his cart and a debris field composed of his totes and the flotsam and jetsam that until a few moments ago had been the new, pristine and unsullied goods that he had most recently picked.

Me: "What happened?"

Jake: "The scanner told me to go to the first floor, but when I tried to push the cart down the steps, everything capsized."

I looked over my shoulder at the conveyor belt literally ten steps away, looked back at Jake, then walked off to find someone slightly less disheartening to talk with.

Perhaps Matt.

Day 63:

There are moments here that are quite pleasant that I look forward to. The fog of incomprehensibility lifts, and for a few short moments, I enjoy working here.

Lunch with the remnants of my training group is one of these moments. There are only five of us left and that has forged a bond between us.

And so we gather at the same table each shift, our own little clique. The initial conversations consistently center around rate, odd items we picked, and unavoided interactions with Matt.

Eventually, we pass on to other topics, each of us gradually presenting the others with the essence of ourselves, and the pictures we paint are invariably colored by our fears.

Riann: a single mother with an eight-month-old worries about her daughter's health (for she is sickly), her inability to find child care most nights, her hesitancy to explain to us what she does when she can't, and her frustration that as a Hispanic woman without a high school degree, The Company is her best employment option this area affords.

Manny: mid-40s, from the Dominican Republic, anxious he will be fired soon since his rate has yet to top 80%. When he is not talking baseball, he is telling us how many weeks he needs to avoid being fired before he can achieve his goal of saving enough money to go back to the Dominican to visit his wife. He needs to get through to the end of November, another six weeks.

Kevin: 22, left a day job at Foot Locker because he hated selling shoes (although his stories of the place make it clear it was not the shoes, but the constant harassment he suffered from his homophobic co-workers). He and his partner were both in our training group, but his partner did not make it three weeks before being fired. Although he does not mention this to us, it is clear Kevin misses him, and is quite lonely.

Jason: 25, African American. As a result of his waywardness as a teen, he has three children from three different mothers. He took this job as a way to get straight and be responsible. He plans to marry that last mother and support his other two kids fully and is saving for a down payment on a house. He contributes to the lunch discussion with either a tally report (like Manny, he is counting down how much longer he needs to work here to achieve his goal) or showing us pictures on his phone of the house he hopes he will soon own.

They, and a few others, humanize this place. Their dreams inoculate them to the rampant dysfunction and the impossibility of this place.

I am in awe of them.

Day 64:

The enforced isolation of this place does lend a certain clarity of thought. For example, today I pondered the oddness of expectant parents, who, when asked if they had a gender preference, say that they just hope the baby has ten fingers and ten toes.

I would have thought that they would be more concerned that it had a head.

Later on, it also occurred to me that if you play a country song backwards, the singer gets all his stuff back.

I think that's nice.

Day 65:

Today, the form of my protest will be haiku:

Yodeling Pickles?
As my soul disintegrates
A mad world buys these.

Day 66:

Tonight, I walked by Mike as he was lifting a 36 lb. bag of dog food into a tote.

"Be careful with that," I told him. "All the weight is on the inside."

He looked at me for a moment, smiled, as if touched by my concern, and said, "Thanks, Paul."

Day 67:

Today, Brad cornered me at stand-up.

He tells me he met a woman over the weekend who's "seriously into me."

He then adds that this woman's 15-year-old daughter sent him a text this morning reading: "I think you're sexy."

He closes with: "So, I'm thinking there's some mother/daughter three-way action coming my way."

I hate this place.

Day 68:

I had a few minutes before lunch break was over, so I went outside and sat on the steps and just enjoyed the silence and the beauty of the night sky.

I saw a shooting star, and remembering my mother always encouraged me to wish upon one, I did so.

I wished for peace throughout the world.

And for a job that did not so closely resemble Hell.

And an Xbox.

Yeah, an Xbox would be sweet.

Day 69:

Shortly after I passed — and once again had my humanity denied — by Lurch, I noticed a pair of 5-inch needle nose pliers in a nearby bin.

Before I knew it, I had the pliers in my hand and was racing after Lurch, thinking to myself "I have ways to make you talk."

If I did not run into Mable and her torture-defusing bag of Dum-Dums, I don't know what would have happened.

There is evil in this place; it leaks into my soul.

Day 70:

Today I picked a bag of hedgehog food. I was dismayed to discover it did not contain gold rings.

My world. It crashes around me.

Day 71:

The language of the Company is one of acronyms: There is V.T.O. (voluntary time off), M.T.O. (mandatory time off), P.T.O. (paid time off), U.P.T. (unpaid personal time), V.O.T. (voluntary overtime), M.O.T. (mandatory overtime), V.C.P. (variable compensation percentage),T.O.T. (time off task), and P.A.s (process assistants).

Now they have introduced V.O.A.: Voice of the Associate.

The idea is to provide a whiteboard where any associate can ask questions or raise concerns with management.

I celebrate this decision. This place thrives on isolation, and depersonalization is its very foundation. Much like convicted felons are issued numbers which become their new identity, many pickers are not known to management by their names, but by their rates. Will (my actual manager) actually greeted me one night with a "Hello, 105," so anything that gives us some voice is a positive move.

I also like that management, we were told, *must* respond to all queries and comments offered through the V.O.A.

Yesterday, I decided to give it a try, offering the following advice:

"Fire Mike"

The response tonight: "Please use this board for legitimate concerns."

As they say, you can lead a horse to water . . .

Day 72:

Undeterred by yesterday's response, I stopped by the P.A. desk before trying the V.O.A. again.

Using Mike's User ID, I wrote "Fire me."

The response: "Ha, ha, Mike. Good One."

This place is beyond help.

Day 73:

As I drove into work tonight, I passed one of the neighborhood dogs vomiting on its owner's driveway.

After a moment to recover, the dog returned to the steaming pile and ingested what it had moments ago disgorged.

As metaphors go, I found it quite apt.

Day 74:

Lurch is not a ghost, a cyborg, or a figment of my progressively-unhinged mind. He's just a kid putting himself through college. And he even has a name: Jakob.

I learned this from Riann, who grew up in the same neighborhood as his family and has known him since they were kids.

The child of Romanian immigrants, he's the first member of his family to go to college. He's a senior majoring in chemical and biomolecular engineering at Lehigh University. His parents were acrobats for Ringling Brothers and Barnum and Bailey Circus for twenty-plus years, and now, twisted, bent, and broken (but, Riann assures me, boisterous and happy — those genes must skip a generation) they subsist on disability and Social Security. Jakob works here after a full day of classes to cover what his scholarship doesn't, and to save up for med school.

His behavior towards me in the Mod is not the result of misanthropy nor an instinctive grasp of my flaws as a person (for I'm basically an asshole), but stems from his obsession (as in reading the *American Journal of Medicine* in his spare time obsession) with finding a cure for muscular dystrophy, which afflicts his younger sister. According to Riann, he's quite confident he'll solve this problem if provided with enough time and resources.

So, when you think about it, I'm not being ignored; I'm providing an essential contribution to curing this horrible disease.

Yeah, I'm one hell of a good person.

That Nobel Prize is gonna look sweet on the mantle.

Day 75:

Mike extended stand-up by fifteen minutes to give all of the pickers training in the new scanner software.

He closed the training by asking: "Does anyone have any questions? Any questions at all?"

I raised my hand.

"Yes, Paul?"

"Am I the only one surprised that Andy Dick is still alive?"

He didn't say anything. He just looked at me for a moment or two, then turned and walked away.

I don't think he likes me very much.

Day 76:

We have a contemptuous hatred of the chicken that borders on the psychotic, a truth clearly indicated by the fact that before we bread it, we first bathe it in the liquefied bodies of its children.

Day 77:

Last week, my fellow workers and I were encouraged to dress up in costumes for our shifts. Seemed like a great way to get into the Halloween spirit.

But we were then told our costumes could have no props. Or masks. Or any garment that was loose fitting. Basically, we could wear t-shirts.

After thinking long and hard about what my costume should

be, I went to my shifts dressed as the T-shirt-wearing-employee-who-is-confused-about-what-the-point-of-the-offer-was.

I was told my costume was quite life-like, so that was nice.

Day 78:

There is a prescribed pathway that pickers use to get from the East Mod to the West Mod. Pickers are *not* to deviate from this path while walking from end to end. This rule is designed to keep us safe from the frenetic forklift traffic all around the warehouse.

Management calls the path from one Hell to another "The Green Mile," because it is outlined in green tape.

I'll take "Unintentional Irony" for $400, Alex.

Day 79:

Matt again.

I am wearing shorts in late November, as I frequently do.

Matt points at my exposed legs: "What do you think it is, summer?"

I give my standard answer to comments like this: "I'm part Viking."

His eyes get wide: "Dude, you don't even have an accent."

I walked away, looking for someone to hug me and tell me it would be ok.

Day 80:

I always find the phrase: "I just threw up in my mouth" to be silly and needlessly redundant.

Unless I've been doing it wrong all these years, every time I throw up, I do it in my mouth.

This type of mental clarity is the best this place has to offer.

Day 81:

When I picked a copy of *The Addams Family* on DVD tonight, it occurred to me that I had not seen Lurch for some time.

When I mentioned this to Riann at lunch, she told me Jakob had been fired a few days ago. Two consecutive weeks of not making rate (two weeks, incidentally, that he was studying for the MCATs), and he was gone. He had been working here for just over two years, and the hundred-plus weeks of hitting rate did not matter; the week he finished at 96% and the following week when he came in at 97% did.

2nd entry:

I was picking "scab colored" band-aids, when I noticed in the adjacent bin several copies of Arthur Miller's *Death of a Salesman*. I thought about Willy Loman's tragic discovery of the sham that is the American Dream.

Then I thought about Jakob's parents, carrying on a centuries-old tradition of leaving their homeland to come to the Land of Opportunity. Where you were told that if you worked hard, you could achieve that American Dream. They did work hard, and for it got disability checks that barely put a roof over their heads and food on their table.

48

Then I thought about Jakob. He also worked hard, up to fifty hours a week on top of carrying a full load of the most unimaginably difficult courses (biomolecular engineering!?!) and for being a combined 7% under rate for 2 weeks, he was fired.

Then I thought about me, and the Nobel Prize I've now lost through no fault of my own.

I grabbed a copy of Miller's play, adding it to the order I was assembling and placed the bin on a conveyor belt.

Some anonymous packer upstairs would remove it, so it was a hollow gesture, an empty idea, like so many others.

I hate this place.

Day 82:

Today I visited the Company's Problem Solve Answer Desk.

I have heard they do great work. At the end of every start-up, Mike always encourages us to bring any questions we have to the Problem Solve Answer Desk and "they will set you straight."

"Why do I keep showing up, every day, to a job that sucks this bad?" I asked.

"Um, what?" the would-be guru asked.

I repeated my question and then explained that we were told the Problem Solve Answer Desk could answer any questions we had.

"I can't answer that question. We only handle work-related questions."

"But this *is* a work-related question," I insisted.

He met this with a blank stare, blinked a few times, and then turned back to his computer, ignoring my repeated "excuse me"s, "hello"s, and assorted throat clearings.

Answer Desk, my ass!

Day 83:

At stand-up, Mike shared a new Company policy that mandates all fingernails and toenails must not exceed ¼" in length.

When he asked if anyone had any questions about the policy, I raised my hand, and while I'm not positive, I think I heard him sigh before he said "Yes, Paul?"

"Will we be subject to random inspections?"

This time I am quite certain he sighed before replying, "I don't know, Paul."

I raised my hand a second time and pushed ahead with my question before any more of that sighing business: "Can we look forward to a policy on pubic hair next?"

He simply stared at me. Deciding to fill the silence with elaboration, I continued: "I'm just asking because I plan on showering later today and if I need to shave, I'd like to know now so I can plan accordingly."

No reply. Just the stare.

I think he thinks I was kidding.

And I don't think he likes me very much.

Day 84:

It is 3:36 a.m.

For the last two grueling, unrelenting hours, several questions have been nagging me, the elusive answers to which threaten me with madness:

Have we figured out who put the "bop" in the "bopshebop," or do we still have people working on this?

Why doesn't Blinds-To-Go have a drive-through?

Does a Muhammad Ali bobblehead doll just stay still?

I may not make it through the night.

Day 85:

And then there were three.

Riann had already been fired. Her daughter was sick one too many times for The Company's taste.

And now Jason is gone.

While I am saddened by this — for he was still a few thousand dollars short of his down payment target — I am not surprised.

Jason does not have a car, and so he gets a ride into work with a friend. When that friend got fired not making rate, Jason only had reliable access to transportation on Sundays and Wednesdays. On Mondays and Tuesdays, he had to catch as catch can, and I know of at least one time that Jason walked the 36 miles from his home in Reading to the warehouse and then slept in a nearby culvert until his weekly shift was over, when he walked home.

Unfortunately for Jason, the Company has rigid block shifts; no individual can tailor a weekly schedule to accommodate minutiae such as access to transportation. If you are hired into a Sunday-Wednesday block, you work Sunday-Wednesday, no exceptions.

And so, because of this refusal to acknowledge workers as individuals with needs and dreams, a dedicated worker (36 miles!) whose rate never dipped below 100% will be forced to discover the answer to that famous question Langston Hughes asked all those years ago: What happens to a dream deferred?

This place sucks.

Day 86:

There is a moment late in *One Flew Over the Cuckoo's Nest* where Chief notices for the first time how tired McMurphy is; the price of taking on the burdens of his charges and trying to teach his fellow patients on the ward how to live without fear, how to survive in a world specifically designed to crush their spirit, is wearing him down.

For the past few weeks, I've noticed the same look on Wendell's face. Tonight, I asked him about it.

"I'm almost at two years."

When I did not immediately respond, he added,

"When my stock vests."

One of the benefits of being converted to a full-timer is that The Company celebrates your new status by awarding you five shares of Company stock.

It's a really nice perk.

The rub is that it does not vest until your two-year anniversary. And the reason that Wendell is considered a veteran here despite just now approaching two years of employment is that very odd things seem to happen to many workers approaching their two-year anniversary.

They seem to suddenly get decidedly-unfriendly pick paths, paths that repeatedly send them from one end of the Mod to the other to make a single pick before sending them back to the other end for the next one. Sometimes they are shifted from East Mod to West Mod several times during a shift. Or they find themselves in Palletland for extended stays. They get harassed about rate, about T.O.T, and about other code violations turned up during suddenly-frequent P.A. visits. And then they seem to get fired. Just before that nice-looking carrot dangled before their eyes for two years is finally theirs.

For all its wonderful PR stunts, this place sucks.

Day 87:

Wanting to understand the scope of the Mods, my wife told me she could see Bay 25 when she drove past the warehouse (there is a hill that hides the warehouse east of this). Using the bay as a landmark, I was able to convey to her some sense of the scale of the place.

Now though, whenever my pick path takes me past Bay 25, I always stop and look through its slats. I know it's goofy of me, but I'm always hoping I'll see her and my two sons standing outside, waving encouragingly.

Of course, they're never there (for it is in the dead of night), just as I'm not there for them during the day (as my broken body recovers, in a state that is more coma than sleep).

I hate this place.

And I want to go home.

Day 88:

Tonight, I passed a bag of Chef Michael's Gourmet Dog Food, and it got me thinking:

Just how bad do you need to fuck up in culinary school before they assign you to the dog food division?

Day 89:

During tonight's post-lunch stand-up, Mike complained that we needed to be sure to stop our carts at the end of the aisle and look both ways before continuing.

In order to impress upon us the severity of this issue, he mentioned that yesterday he was run into by carts at least four times and today his shins really hurt.

I observed that "maybe the problem is not systemic, but personal."

He gave me a blank stare for a few beats before replying, "Paul, I have no idea what you mean by 'systemic.'"

Pulling the hood of my sweatshirt over my head to enhance the Jedi-like tone I was going for, I offered in return: "That, dear sir, is why it may be personal."

Then I slowly backed into the Mod with a finger across my lips.

Day 90:

I passed that bag of Gourmet Dog Food again, and as this long night progresses, I find myself thinking more about the tragedy that is Chef Michael.

How fulfilling can it be for him, I think to myself, to express his love of food preparation for a consumer that spends 4-6 hours on average licking its own ass?

Cry for Chef Michael. Cry for us all.

Day 91:

Manny is becoming increasingly frightened of being fired.

"I can't lose this job," he cried as we stopped for a quick chat in the Mod. "No place around here pays as well. With one of those jobs, it'll take me a year to save enough to fly home."

I never challenged Manny as to why it should take that long to save for a $500 plane ticket; I noted that Manny ate a lunch of white bread with margarine every night, and assumed that his paycheck must be consumed by rent and utilities, leaving virtually nothing left to save.

"How do you keep your rate so high?" he asked me.

"Well, for one thing, I don't spend so much time looking at the product."

"What do you mean?"

"Manny, I've watched you pick a few times. You spend minutes looking at stuff, reading the labels. I've seen you read pages of a book you were picking. You then look at the other stuff in the bin. That's probably why your rate is so low."

"But it's all so fascinating to me, the stuff for sale in America."

I immediately thought of the Yodeling Pickle, and could not disagree with him.

O, brave new world that has such things in it.

But Manny, I fear, may be doomed.

Day 92:

I am beginning to feel bad about the pariah status forced onto The Masturbator based solely on his obsessive need for self-defilement.

Tonight, I decided I would no longer indulge in this particular strain of GroupThink, and so when our pick paths intersected, I said "hello" and we briefly chatted. His name was Chad; he seemed like a perfectly normal person and at no point during our discussion did I get the sense he was mentally counting the minutes before he could indulge in another bout of manual pleasure.

Ultimately, curiosity got the better of me: "I gotta ask, why do you do it?"

His face sunk for a second, recognizing there was no need to ask what the "it" was. He took a moment to answer, as if evaluating whether I could possibly understand.

"Boredom," he replied at last.

"Come again?"

"I just get so fucking bored here. Jerking off seems like as good a way as any to kill some time."

There are many legitimate charges one can throw at The Company's famous C.E.O., but tonight I've discovered perhaps his greatest crime: sucking the joy out of masturbation, rendering it merely something one does "to pass the time."

That man (and this place) are truly evil.

Day 93:

Mike has just announced that due to a Next Day shipping backlog, our lunch break has been pushed back to 1:30 instead of the customary midnight.

It is now 1:08 in the morning.

Hunger ravages me.

The pick path I'm on has taken me past the bag of Chef Michael's Gourmet Dog Food nine times in the last thirty minutes.

I feel my resistance failing.

It is only a matter of time before I cave and sample Chef Michael's offerings, and lose what little humanity I have left.

Day 94:

I try really hard not to make assumptions about the people who place the orders I pick, but sometimes this proves quite difficult.

Today, I filled an order consisting of *Co-Ed Sluts 5* on DVD, and a 7.5 oz bottle of Jergens lotion. That part of the order was hardly uncommon (stay classy, America!). But the addition of a 16 oz. bag of coffee did raise an eyebrow.

Perhaps a hedge against the erotic quality of the porn? Is this customer Chad's antipode? Or just someone planning a marathon session? Was the selection of Chock Full O' Nuts whimsy or unintentionally ironic?

Day 95:

Since I've been here, I've made some odd picks (see: Yodeling Pickle).

But I must say the Vegan jerky is an item of particular semantic ridiculousness.

It's fairly simple: If you opt to go Vegan, you have opted out of jerky.

It's a mutually-exclusive situation: If there's no meat, it is not jerky. It's just a stick.

Day 96:

Thanksgiving is a holiday where families gather and share what it is they are thankful for. I think this is a great tradition. I'm working, so I'm not with my family tonight, but here goes:

I'm thankful that tonight marks the start of Peak Season, where my hellish ten-hour shift walking fifteen-eighteen miles a night four consecutive nights comes to an end, replaced by hellish twelve-hour shifts walking eighteen-twenty-two miles a night five consecutive nights. I can hardly wait.

I am thankful that the management here is celebrating the holiday by serving us a Thanksgiving dinner with all the trimmings (to be gobbled down in the twenty-five-minute lunch break window), even if Mike is not wearing the required plastic gloves. I didn't really want those delicious looking dinner rolls anyway.

I *was* thankful for holiday pay, until Mike informed us that those of us who are typically scheduled to work Thursday nights won't be getting holiday pay, since this is a normal work day for us. It's only money, after all.

It suddenly occurs to me that if it wasn't for Mabel celebrating by handing out Blow-Pops instead of her normal Dum-Dums, this holiday would be a complete failure.

I think I hate Thanksgiving.

Day 97:

The Company unveiled a new motivational slogan for peak season.

Posted over the entryway to the factory floor (replacing the one that read *Lasciate ogne speranza, voi ch'intrate*) is a sign extolling us to:

Work Hard. Have Fun. Make History.

I find the last part of the message to be quite silly.

There are many words I could use to describe a night picking yodeling pickles and One Direction CDs, but "historic" is not one of them.

"Hellish" perhaps.

Possibly "miserable."

Certainly "dismal."

But not "historic."

Because this place sucks.

And so does that slogan.

Day 98:

A few days ago, The Company's C.E.O. made headlines with his promise that soon he would employ an army of drones to deliver products to the customer's door within an hour.

At first I, like many, noted the impossibility of this and chalked the comment up to a clever publicity stunt.

But as I look about me tonight, and see the hundreds of workers wandering the Mod, mindlessly responding to the orders of a computer program, I think to myself: the army of drones is already here, and I am of it.

I hate this place.

Day 99:

There is comfort in routine.

A point brought home to me today when I approached my usual table and found several new hires had claimed the chairs that had so recently held the final holdouts of my training group.

Manny has been the latest to go, finally fired for rate.

Kevin then started sitting with a new group of friends he's made. I kept sitting at our table out of habit. Until tonight.

Rather than intruding on other people's routines and comfort zones, I took my lunch outside and sat on the entry steps and thought about Manny.

I really hope he finds his way home to his wife.

And I really hate this place.

Day 100:

I live in a Bizarro world, devoid of logic. This is the only explanation possible for the following conversation with Mike:

Mike: "We're gonna really beat up Walmart and Toys R Us this Christmas season."

Me: "Why's that?"

Mike: "In our call with corporate, they told us we're undercutting them on prices. We're going to sell certain items at below cost to ensure people buy those items from us."

Me: "We're going to sell stuff for less than we paid for it?"

Mike: "Exactly!"

Me: "How does one make money selling something for *less* than one paid for it?"

Mike (wagging his finger at me knowingly): "Volume!"

Somewhere in the Congo, Charlie Marlow waits for his rivets.

I know how he feels.

Day 101:

I've been giving this new motivational slogan a lot of thought. And the V.O.A. seemed like the place to offer a nuanced revision.

My idea: "I suggest we change the company slogan from 'Work Hard. Have Fun. Make History.' to 'I No Longer Fear Hell, Because I Work Here.'"

The response: "Ha!"

I think they think I'm joking.

Day 102:

On Cyber Monday overnight, we shipped more than 500,000 units — a new record for the facility.

To celebrate, and to build on the good will they created with us after their fingernail/toenail policy, management announced today that certain bathrooms (the single stall, unisex ones with locking doors at the end of each Mod) will be for urination only.

Mike said (with a completely straight face) "if you need to take a B.M., use the multi-stall bathrooms located in the center of the warehouse."

He also suggested that we time our visits to coincide with our breaks.

I intended to ask if corporate would soon be announcing a policy on how much toilet paper we should use per visit, but I guess Mike forgot to put his contacts in tonight, since he did not see my raised, then frantically-waving, hand.

The sound of the conveyor belt must have drowned out my repeated "Excuse me"s as well.

But mostly, I'm concerned how this policy will impact Chad.

Day 103:

For all of my grousing, there *are* a few perks of working here.

For example, prior to five straight twelve-hour shifts, my understanding of the word "comatose" was purely theoretical.

Another advantage is that picking in the Mods affords me the opportunity to stumble across Christmas gift ideas for my family. Just the other night, I discovered a neat martini glass that I know my wife would like. The only problem is that typically I am so exhausted by the time I get home that I have long since forgotten most of the finds I made that shift.

I mentioned to Mike tonight that I was a little surprised we did not have the opportunity to simply purchase items here at the end of our shift.

"We'd never be able to handle the logistics of something like that," Mike dismissively replied.

I looked down at my scanner, which can instantly compile a pick path for me and time each pick to the second.

I then considered the thousands of bar code readers across the factory, allowing any specific item's location to be pin-pointed at any given moment.

I then looked overhead at the miles of conveyor belts snaking around the factory, transmitting a ceaseless flow of specific items to a specific packer waiting to put them into a specific box, which is then conveyed to a specific pallet to be loaded onto a specific truck to be transported to a specific post office to be hand-delivered to a specific address, all calibrated to the Company's mandate of delivery within forty-eight hours from purchase.

I then looked back at Mike.

"Yeah, I know what you mean."

Day 104:

Management is trying to break Angry Man.

I know this because I ran into him deep in the East Mod late tonight.

In my surprise, I blurted out "What the hell are you doing here?"

While it's not the best idea to open conversation with someone with acute anger management issues and possible psychopathic leanings with provoking questions, Angry Man is a Packer, and so had no business in the Mods.

Also, Pickers and Packers do not get along.

Packers work upstairs, on the receiving end of the conveyor belts that snake through the Mods. Instead of walking for twelve-hours straight, Packers get to stand in place for twelve-hours straight; and instead of having hand-held scanners time their every move, they get large computer monitors to do that.

Packers have it easy.

We basically hate them.

Angry Man: "I'm a Picker now."

Me: "Why on Earth would you want to move to Pick?"

Angry Man: "I didn't. I got sent here. As punishment."

Me: "Come again?"

Angry Man: "I was falling way off rate because I had to keep

63

sitting down. My feet were hurting so bad from standing all night, every night. When the P.A. barked at me about it, well, I don't know if you know this, but I have some anger issues."

Me: "Really? Hadn't noticed."

Angry Man: "Yeah, so I got a little heated. And then next shift, they told me I was now a Picker."

I must say I am not thrilled to find out that the job I have is considered "punishment" by management.

And I must also say that if Angry Man's feet were breaking down as a Packer, he has no shot at surviving as a Picker.

And I must further say that this place sucks.

2nd entry:

As I limped out of the Mod at shift's end, I noticed Angry Man. He was not so much walking as shuffling, pain etched into his face. When one of his antagonist Mets fans walked past him, Angry Man didn't even notice. He's already a broken man.

As we got in line for Security's metal detectors, I placed my hand on his arm, and said, "Your leg muscles will stabilize in about a week's time. Hang in there, and your body will adjust."

Angry Man's face softened a little and he gave me a wan smile. He then extended his hand.

"My name is Sam."

I took his hand and shook it.

"Hi, Sam. I'm Paul."

Day 105:

Brad (*sotto voce*): "Hey, do you ever get the chance to pick a sex toy?"

64

Me (since during the average shift I pick about a dozen—stay classy, America): "Um, yes. Why?"

Brad: "Do you ever touch them? You know, feel them?"

Me: "Considering that the normal performance of a picker's job involves physically picking up an item and physically placing it in a tote, I think such manual interactions are unavoidable."

Brad: "Huh?"

Me (sigh): "Yes, Brad. I touch them. To get them in the tote."

Brad furtively looks around to be sure there is no one to overhear us. Then:

"Sometimes I like to sneak them into the bathrooms (I assume the single stall, piss-only, ones at the end of the Mods) and use them. You know, try them out. So I know if they're worth buying."

Other than making a mental note to warn all my friends, family, and associates that if they were planning on buying a loved one a sex toy for Christmas (and, really, what says "Deck the Halls" more than a Jeff Stryker 10" dildo with suction cup base?), they should perhaps do their shopping elsewhere, I did not know what to do or say to this piece of unsolicited information.

Except throw up a little. In my mouth.

Day 106:

I haven't seen Wendell in quite some time. I hope he's O.K.

Day 107:

Mabel has not been her psychotically cheerful self lately. She still hands out the Dum-Dums, but she does so mechanically and without the kind words that are her true currency.

As near as I can tell, the attitude change stems from Mike. It's clear that the increased physical demands of Peak Season are taking a toll on Mabel and Mike's been riding her ass hard lately about barely making rate.

I can put up with the impossibility that is this place, the mind-numbing conversations with Matt, the near-crippling foot pain, even Mike doing his Major Burns thing, but as God is my witness, if my lollipop connection gets messed up, I will burn this fucking place to the ground.

Day 108:

Mike was not in a good mood at stand-up.

Allegedly, someone stole his Tastykake during lunch.

The story goes that he got up to grab some napkins and when he returned, his Krimpets were gone. In their place was a hastily scrawled note on a napkin that read:

"Bring a dollar to the old oak tree tomorrow or the pastry gets it! Do not involve the authorities!"

I think he suspects I had something to do with it.

Day 109:

Movies have played a big role in my life.

Kramer vs. Kramer provided solace and understanding during my parents' divorce.

Mr. Holland's Opus offered perspective when I would get frustrated that my teaching career did not leave me any time to write.

And *The Amityville Horror* taught me that when a house says "Get out!" I should probably just get the fuck out.

And now, in the midst of the winter of my discontent, my love of film is once again trying to comfort me, by way of a co-worker named Brian.

A perpetually-smiling man in his mid-50s, Brian in a previous life worked at the El Rey Inn in Santa Fe, rubbing elbows with movie stars such as Robert De Niro, John Malkovich, Ali MacGraw, Vincent Price, and Arnold Schwarzenegger.

Learning of my love of movies, Brian one night challenged me as we crossed pick paths to name the three Westerns to win an Oscar for Best Picture. Since that night, when we're working in the same section, we bombard each other with movie trivia or play rounds of movie quote identification.

The value of this mental stimulation cannot be understated. Nights when I work with Brian go by quicker and I feel like a thinking human being. I drive to work on Mondays and Tuesdays (the only nights our schedules overlap) with something akin to hope.

The games Brian and I play leave me with a bittersweet feeling, for they highlight the fact that I have very little time — and during that time I do not have the energy — to watch movies anymore. Although last night, I picked a new release called *Wolf Children*, which, near as I can tell, is a film about how to raise little werewolves.

So maybe it's a good thing I have no time to watch movies anymore.

Day 110:

Mike asked for volunteers to go do some gift-wrapping. I immediately raised my hand, shouting "I'm great at rapping!" I dropped a little human beat-box on him and then followed with some freestyle bombs.

I thought I really brought the house down, but all Mike said was, "Paul, get back to work."

He then picked someone else.

I don't think he likes me very much.

Day 111:

The consensus amongst the few veterans I talk to regularly is that if I thought a typical shift was Freak Show Central, I ain't seen nothing yet.

The flood of temporary workers that signals the beginning of peak season will introduce me, I've been told, to a whole new cast of even more impossibly bizarre individuals.

I met the first of those tonight.

Jimmy, a tall, gangly, flamboyantly-dressed African American man in his mid-40s who looked disconcertingly like the Muppet Mr. Teeth. Charismatic and loquacious, I liked him immediately and began to share with him various tricks of the trade I've picked up over the past few months.

"Oh, I know the score," he interrupted. "I worked here last peak season for about four weeks until I got fired."

"Oh. What happened?"

"Me and a lady friend got caught getting busy"

"Holy shit! That was you?!?" (For this story, which I had always assumed was apocryphal, was legendary in the Mods.)

"Yeah," Jimmy grinned sheepishly, the factory florescent lights glinting off his gold tooth. "That was me. And I was here the summer before that for about three weeks before I got canned."

"For?"

"Same thing."

Fulfillment center, indeed, I thought as I resumed my pick path. Fulfillment center indeed.

Day 112:

Discussed Jimmy with Kevin during lunch.

"What staggers me most about this," I offered, "is not that this guy got fired for shagging someone in a Mod aisle, *twice*. But that he is here again. What kind of fucked up company hires back someone they've already fired twice within the last sixteen months?"

"There's actually a policy covering rehires," Kevin said.

When I got home, I consulted my employment manual (which is interestingly called the Owner's Manual) and, sure enough, there is indeed a policy for it.

Employees who have been terminated for any reason other than theft must wait forty-five days before they re-apply.

So, in essence, if you misbehave at The Company or you're a shitty employee, you do not get fired; you get a time out.

Day 113:

Today Mabel asked if I would tell Brad to stop telling her crude, dirty jokes.

"Why?" I asked.

"Because they make me feel uncomfortable."

"No, why me? Why not go to HR?"

"I did."

"And?"

"The Sarge told me I have a nice ass, for an 'older gal.'"

This place sucks.

Day 114:

Most nights, I now eat with Sam in the cafeteria, and I must admit I enjoy having someone to talk with during lunch breaks again. Since my training group scattered, I've been without the little slice of camaraderie it provided and didn't realize how much I missed it.

During this time, I've learned a bit of Sam's story, a story that explains to some degree Angry Man.

When Sam is not working here, he is taking care of his physically- and mentally-handicapped younger brother. With whatever time he has left, he goes to his ailing mother's house and helps there. Somewhere in that schedule, he squeezes in a bit of sleep. Sam would like to get married and start a family of his own, but at 48, thinks he's missed that boat.

"Plus," he told me one night, "when do I have time to date? And how do I bring a woman home to a one-bedroom apartment I share with my brother?"

I'm having a hard time reconciling Sam's daily routine of good deeds, his soft-spokenness at lunch, and his friendship with the rage I've seen him erupt into.

So tonight I asked him point blank:

Me: "Sam, were you ever exposed to large doses of gamma rays?"

Sam: "No, man. What the fuck are you talking about?"

Me: "Nothing. Never mind."

I think he's lying about the gamma rays. Sometimes when the light in the cafeteria catches him just right, I think I can see Angry Man lurking behind those eyes, waiting to come out.

I want to stay on his good side, so I tonight I gave him a pack of Tastycake Krimpets.

They weren't mine anyway.

Day 115:

There are many things here that horrify me.

Most of them involve Brad.

Tonight, I have to add the janitor to the list.

I was about four aisles away from him when I decided — since it was early in the shift and I was in a decent mood and relatively pain-free — to help him by grabbing a full trash can with the intention of carrying it over to him.

The Janitor: "I'm the janitor!"

Me: "I know. I just wanted to help."

The Janitor: "I'm the janitor!"

Me: "O.K."

The Janitor (pointing at the spot on the floor where the trash can was before I picked it up): "I'm the janitor!"

Seeing his evident distress, I replaced the trash can. He hobbled over to it, snatched it up, emptied it into his bag, and moved up the aisle.

"Sorry," I called to him.

"I'm the janitor," he replied.

There is horror in these three words. I'm just not sure what the horror actually is.

Is this refrain an expression of warped pride?

Or has his humanity been so subsumed into his job description that this is the only identity he acknowledges?

Or is this the sum total of his verbal range? If so, how does he function outside of the warehouse? How in the hell does he order carry-out?

Does his mental voice have the same restrictions? Are his thoughts limited to this existentially-stagnant mœbius strip?

Did this place do this to him?

I do not know the answers to these questions.

What I do know is that I need to get out of here.

Fast.

Day 116:

As I prepare for my second week of peak season hell, I take some time to reflect on what I learned during the first week:

1. Using the average mileage a picker hitting their 100% rate for an twelve-hour shift walks (19.6 miles), I now know what it is like to walk to Maryland and I know I can do it in about five days.

2. I know (to my profound dismay) that I live in a world where there is not only a *Nickleback's Greatest Hits* CD, but one embellished with the following threat: "Volume One."

What joys await me this week?

Day 117:

In the last half an hour, I've walked past Brad as he thoroughly inspects a Healthy Vibes Pocket Vagina, crossed an aisle where Jimmy was sweet-talking another seasonal worker, furtively gauging their level of privacy, and noted Chad heading into the single stall bathroom at (as a glance at my scanner confirmed) 11:40, right as rain.

The warehouse has never been sexier.

Day 118:

Today's interaction with Mike:

I stride over to his desk, slam down a can of Alpo dog food, and, beaming my best grin, proudly announce:

"It's in the can," tapping the lid for extra clarification. "I'm guessing 'in the can.' Am I right? Do I get an iPad?"

Confusion barely edged out the "Good Lord, here we go again" look on Mike's face.

"I'm not following you, Paul."

I pointed to the label on the can that read "Hidden Goodness Dog Food."

Since this did not seem to clear things up for Mike, I explained:

"At first I was just going to scan the can and put it in the tote, but then I got to thinking: 'What a dumb name for a product.' I mean, if you hide something, the worst thing you can do is announce you hid it; gets everyone looking for it and all. I remember a sign for a town named Hidden Valley in New Jersey, and they had it right there on a road sign — "Hidden Valley, 8 miles" — with an arrow pointing to the right.

73

At first I thought it was a ruse, but no. I took the right (even though it was out of my way) and sure enough, eight miles down the road there it is. If your valley is supposed to be hidden, I think it's pretty foolish to post directions to it.

Anyway, this got me thinking about how you said during stand-up that The Company runs contests for the workers during peak season, giving out iPads and such. So the way I figure it is, this is one of those contests; you know, a 'Guess where the Goodness is hidden' kinda thing?

Seeing as you're a shifty one, I went into the coat room and rifled through your coat pockets, thinking you may have hidden the Goodness there. All I found was a partially-used roll of Chap Stick — and I hope you don't mind that I used some; the warehouse sure does get dry in winter — and an Andes mint. I unwrapped it; it looks pretty old and stale, although the corner I nibbled on tasted fine. You may want to eat the rest fairly soon.

But then it hit me!

It's in the can! So obvious when you think of it. Anyway, my answer is:

'Alpo hid the Hidden Goodness Dog Food in the can of dog food.'

So, I'm right? I'm right, aren't I? I'm getting an iPad."

After a few moment's pause, during which he rubbed his face with both hands and muttered something under his breath that sounded a lot like "I skate is ducking fly" — which makes *no* sense — he replied,

"No, Paul. You're not getting an iPad. Please get back to work."

I think he's lying. I think he's going to submit *my* answer as his and steal my iPad.

I also think he doesn't like me very much.

74

Day 119:

A few minutes before the shift began, Matt was sitting in the break area, watching highlights of the Baltimore Ravens' victory over the Steelers earlier today. As ESPN showed the Pittsburgh sideline, Matt began to chant "Over-rated."

Knowing I was courting madness, I mentioned that I found this a bizarre chant.

"It doesn't make any sense."

"Well," Matt countered, "it does. Because Pittsburgh *is* over-rated."

"Yes, but your evidence of that fact is that your team can beat them. What the chant really says is 'You must not be as good as everyone thought if *we* can beat you.' I think a more appropriate chant would be 'We're slightly better.'"

Matt was silent for a moment. Fool that I was, I thought there was a real breakthrough.

But then . . .

"Yeah, well Pittsburgh can go suck it! 'Cause we beat those over-rated chumps."

I wash my hands of the man.

Day 120:

I continue to plumb depths of suffering I did not know were possible.

Picking items for a twelve-hour night shift is brutal enough, but try doing it with a Gordon Lightfoot song stuck in your head.

Day 121:

Morale was down in the Mods; pickers were grumbling about mandatory overtime and the prospect of thirteen-hour shifts. Something had to be done.

Then I arrived at bin B2-H145 and saw a 1-quart saucepan sharing space with a steel rod, and I knew just what to do. Grabbing the pan, I paraded down the aisle, banged on it with the rod at intervals, and called out:

"Bring out your dead."

Alas, not a single person laughed.

Fuck these people.

This place sucks.

Day 122:

At stand-up, I saw one of the temporary workers, who was clearly having scanner troubles, approach me.

"You look like a nice guy," he began.

"Eat a bag of shit," I interrupted. I then knocked his scanner to the floor and walked away.

I think I taught the lad a valuable lesson about the importance of never judging a book by its cover.

Day 123:

One of the most frustrating moments in a child's life is when their well-thought-out and eminently reasonable positions are countered by a parent's dismissive "Because I said so" response.

Having long since reached adulthood, I had assumed that I was now free and clear of the "Because I said so" argument.

But I was wrong. I work for The Company.

For example, when an item I'm supposed to pick is not in the indicated bin, I am required to scan each and every item in that bin to prove to my computer overlord that I am not in fact a dumbass.

This takes time: anywhere between thirty-five seconds to two minutes, depending on the size of the bin and on how densely it's packed. I know it takes this long because my scanner continues to count down my allotted time to find the item even though I have already indicated it is not here. Things that cost time threaten rate numbers, and things that threaten rate numbers threaten employment.

Me: "But why do I have to scan *every single* item? I was asked to pick a DVD. It is painfully obvious, simply by looking into the bin, that there is not a single DVD of *any* kind in the bin."

The Company: "Because I said so."

Me: "If there is a dozen of a single item, like rolls of Scotch tape, why do I have to scan all twelve when I'm looking for, say, bacon-printed Band-Aids, not Scotch tape?"

The Company: "Because I said so."

Me: "Why is my job so soul-crushingly hellish?"

The Company: "Because I said so."

I hate this place.

Day 124:

Sometimes I worry about the things Sam says to me.

Sam: "You know, it's just a matter of time until someone here snaps and goes postal."

Me: "Yeah, I've often wondered how there hasn't been a mass shooting here yet. Particularly when Mike is working."

Sam: "You want to know what I would do if I was going to shoot up this place?

Me: "Um, reconsider?"

Sam: "No, man. I'd do it during lunch break. With most of the shift concentrated in this room, think of all the people you could take out."

When I didn't reply, he added:

Sam: "Don't worry, man. If I'm ever going to do something like that, I'll give you a heads-up that you might want to go out for lunch."

Me: "Thank you, Sam."

Boy am I glad I gave him those Krimpets.

Day 125:

Tonight, a co-worker showed up wearing a red-and-white vertical striped shirt, blue pants, round-rimmed glasses, and a stocking cap

I ran up to him and yelled "There you are! I've been looking all over for you!"

Day 126:

I had a dream that I entered an aisle only to find Brad swinging a double-sided dildo over his head like it was some flesh-colored phallic lasso while declaring, "It's girth that matters."

Then I realized that this was not a dream, it was just a Tuesday.
I hate this place.

Day 127:

Wynton Marsalis' *Christmas Jazz Jam* is an awesome CD.

Unless you don't like jazz.

Or Christmas.

In which case, you may just want to listen to something else.

Day 128:

Even though it has a profoundly harmful impact on my physical and mental well-being, there are times when I simply marvel at The Company's ability to craft new levels of torment.

To accommodate parking needs for all of the seasonal hires, The Company opens up a secondary parking lot about a quarter of a mile away from the factory. A rotation of buses shuttles workers to the facility.

They only run two buses, though.

There are upwards of 1,000 workers during a peak-season shift.

At the end of a twelve-hour shift, few people feel like waiting ten minutes unsheltered in the cold, the piercing wind, the snow for the next bus.

And so, we walk to the overflow lot.

Because, hey, after walking twenty-three miles already that night, what's another quarter mile?

Oh, and it's uphill. Why the hell wouldn't it be uphill?

I hate this place.

Day 129:

Feeling the palpable stress and tension in the air as peak season continues, I desperately want to lift the spirit of my peoples.

Two hours into the shift, in the West Mod's bin C1 D24, I saw how.

Donning the latex hippopotamus mask (and really, why wouldn't somebody produce, package, market, and sell latex hippopotamus masks?), I wandered the Mod, calling out:

"I'm so hungry! Does anyone have some marbles?"

No one laughed, for they are a joyless people incapable of mirth.

Day 130:

Tonight, Mike sent me to do paper picks. A paper pick is when a box is packed but is missing one item (overlooked or sent up damaged), so they write the location down on paper and send a runner to the Mods to get it and rush it back to the packer.

I'll do this for twelve hours.

After he explains it to me, I said, "So, I'm basically playing fetch? Like a dog."

"Um, yeah, I guess you could look at it that way."

"Do I get treats?"

"What?"

"Treats. Like dogs and dolphins do. Anchovies or biscuits. I'd prefer anchovies, but dog biscuits could work. Just not the green ones. Those suck."

Rubbing his face with his hands, he replied "No, Paul. You do not get treats. Just do it."

"But dolphins get treats."

"But we don't use dolphins for this; we use people. Like you."

"I'm not surprised. Dolphins wouldn't work under these no-treat conditions."

"Just get to work, Paul!"

I turned to go, but then I was struck by another thought. "Would you at least rub my belly when I return with the pick?"

"What the hell are you talking about!" Mike shouted (He's been doing this a lot lately. Must be peak-season stress getting to him).

"C'mon, man. I'll do that leg thing."

"Paul, go!"

"Pat my head maybe?"

"JUST GET TO WORK!!"

This place sucks.

And I don't think he likes me very much.

Day 131:

It has been brought to my attention that singing "Massa Got Me Working" while picking is frowned upon by this establishment.

Apparently, "Swing Low, Sweet Chariot" is also out.

How will I survive this if I am not allowed to sing the songs of my peoples?

Day 132:

I think it's awesome that one can buy gift cards from The Company for other stores (Game Stop or Applebee's, for example).

There is nothing like being too lazy to shop when you're already being too lazy to shop.

Day 133:

Undaunted by my failure a few days ago, I once again attempted to lighten the mood of this place.

From one bin, I grabbed a Batman mask and put it on.

From another, a straw sombrero.

I then resumed picking, greeting my peoples with a *"Me llamo Bat hombre"* when we passed.

To mix things up a bit, I would occasionally throw out (in my best Christian Bale I-need-a-throat-lozenge voice) *"De donde Rachel!?!"*

I also yelled *"el perro es grande y negro,"* because, why not?

I was having a bit more success than the Hungry, Hungry, Hippo bit. That is, I *was* until Mike showed up.

"Paul, what the hell are you doing!?" he yelled (see?).

"Having fun."

Mike's blank stare seemed to require some elaboration.

"It's the new peak season slogan. You know: 'Work Hard. Have Fun. Make' —look, it's the second one, dammit! Aren't we supposed to have fun? 'Cause I gotta tell you, this (pointing at the mask/sombrero ensemble) is *fun!*"

After a moment or two of silence, Mike replied: "We don't really mean it."

This place sucks.

Day 134:

One of the more fucked up aspects of the Peak Season parking situation is that many people will voluntarily show up well before shift starts in order to get a spot on the lower lot and avoid the shuttle bus.

Coming in fifteen minutes earlier than usual was initially good enough, but as more people tried to circumvent the bus, a temporal arms race began.

There are now some people who show up an hour and a half before shift and just sit in their cars or in the break room.

Sometimes I wonder if my peoples and I truly exist. Or are we just characters in a Tennessee Ernie Ford song or a Steinbeck novel?

Day 135:

My feet hurt.

I mean *really* hurt.

But not as much as my brain hurts after the conversation I just had with a co-worker.

Me: "I gotta tell you, I can't stand the Elf on the Shelf thing."

83

Her: "I know. Those things creep me out. I could never have one. It would freak me out too much when it moved."

Me (After a confused pause): "Wait, what?"

Her: "I'm just saying I'd be scared knowing it was moving around the house."

Me: "Um, *you* would move it. It's not a real elf."

Her: "I know that silly, it's a robot elf."

Me: "No. No, it's not a robot elf either. It's a plush toy that you move to create delight for small children and to annoy the shit out of your Facebook friends."

Her (sounding quite disappointed): "Oh. Guess I can get one then."

And with that, she walked away.

Me? I sat on a pallet and cried.

I hate this place.

Day 136:

One of the problems with working peak season hours is I don't have much time for typical holiday season activities, such as writing Christmas cards, so tonight, I penned a brief holiday missive during lunch break that I shall send to all my friends and family:

Dear friends and family,

This festive season I offer the following advice to those who may be using The Company for your holiday shopping:

If you receive your order and it actually contains the items you requested — and they are not damaged — you should do the following:

a)offer up a prayer of thanksgiving to whichever deity you deem worthy of worship, and

b)immediately sanitize the item(s) and anything it/they may reasonably have come in contact with. Taken as a whole, my co-workers are a dim-witted, cretinous, hygienically-challenged bunch of social misfits of questionable mental stability.

They believe the Elf on the Shelf is a sentient being; they voluntarily elect to be a one-man Quality Control Department for sex toys; they show each other their abscesses; they pop whitehead zits in the Mods and then resume picking; they do the one-nostril-closed snot blow into trash cans; they are unable to find section D despite standing in section C, and I won't even discuss what they do to the bathrooms.

I would not rely on anti-bacterial soap or hand-sanitizing gels. You may want to consider using a blow torch.

Please understand that this advice is offered to you all in lieu of an actual Christmas gift.

You're welcome.

As far as capturing the holiday spirit, I think Tiny Tim's got nothing on me!

Day 137:

In the last half an hour, I've picked the DVDs *Nursing Home Orgy* and *Bang a Midget* # 2.

There is truly no hope for us.

Day 138:

There are workers here (and not just a few) who bust their ass to reach 180% of rate, an achievement for which they receive no extra bonus, unless you count the occasional awarding of something called Company Bucks — repurposed Monopoly money that they can then exchange, once they have enough, for a beach ball, Frisbee, or a visor emblazoned with The Company logo (so they never forget who owns their souls).

Yet at the end of every quarter shift, there they are, inspecting the rate sheets and squealing in unmerited delight should their name appear at the top of the list.

These are the same fuckers who hide the scanners with the shoulder straps, because they feel the three nanoseconds they save by having the scanner at hand's reach (rather than having to grab it from the holder attached to the cart, like the rest of the unwashed masses do), is the key to such high rate scores.

Sometimes it is really hard for me to care about my peoples.

Day 139:

There's a disproportionate number of gay and lesbian employees here.

I asked Kevin why he thought this was.

"It's safe," he replied. "Think about it. The entire system here denies the humanity of its workers. Policies prevent socialization. Our names and identities are not important; our rate is. In any system that denies identity to all, no one particular identity can be marginalized. Here, we're all dehumanized equally."

On the drive home, I thought of that last sentence of Kevin's:

"Here, we're all dehumanized equally." A more precise slogan than "Work Hard, Have Fun, Make History."

A more precise slogan indeed.

So is: "This place sucks."

Day 140:

If someone wants to buy a toy plastic bag, what the hell do we wrap it in?

Day 141:

There's an old woman here who carries around a bag of Werther's candies and offers you one when she sees you (whether she is copying Mabel or if this is a case of divergent evolution, I can't say). I found this somewhat endearing and always gratefully accepted the proffered candy.

That is, until she made the yummy noise.

I was bending over to reach into a floor-level bin when I heard the yummy noise.

Looking back over my shoulder I saw her eyes locked on my ass.

"Delicious," she said.

She then extended the bag.

What was once a kind and genial gesture now had a sordid, Grimm's Brothers' feel to it.

"No thanks," I said.

"Simply delicious," she repeated, running her tongue across her lips once, before turning away.

I feel dirty. I feel cheap, but most of all, I feel stupid for not taking the scrumptious caramel candy.

I've sold my body for far less.

Day 142:

I suspect Mike does not think I'm a very good worker.

I tried to change that impression tonight.

It did not go well.

As I returned from break this evening, I noticed a Gaylord — one of thousands of eight-foot-tall cardboard boxes used for various storage purposes placed throughout the factory — with a sign on it reading: "Inactive Gaylord."

Recalling that the first directive of our new peak season motivational slogan is "Work Hard," I was upset by this lazy Gaylord brazenly defying The Company's will.

Time, I thought, to bring in Mike.

Me: "We have a problem."

Mike: "What's wrong *now*, Paul?"

While I did not really care for that "now" part, I pressed on.

Me: "There's an inactive Gaylord, just being all inactive and stuff. Right dead-smack in the middle of the factory floor, too. Where everyone can see."

Mike: "Paul, I have no idea what you're talking about."

Me: "I'm talking about the Inactive Gaylord. Over there. We're supposed to 'Work Hard' and 'Make History' and shit like that, but that Gaylord just sits there, inactive. I tried to straighten it out. I yelled 'Get to work, Gaylord,' and 'Stop being so inactive!' and stuff like that, but it just kept on standing there. Doing nothing. So shameless, it even had a sign bragging about

88

how inactive it was being."

Mike blinked at me silently for a few beats.

Me: "Fucking Gaylord!"

Mike: "Paul, please. Please. Please, Paul, just get back to work."

I don't think he understands the situation. Not at all.

Day 143:

Tonight, as I picked a 128-oz bottle of Spunk lubricant, a rapid-fire sequence of thoughts shot through my mind.

Thought One: Stay classy, America. Stay classy.

Thought Two: Holy Crap! That's a *gallon* of lube!

Thought Three: Who in the hell would buy a *gallon* of lube!?!

Later in my shift, as I limped down the Green Mile, I noted that Brad was chatting with The Sarge at the latter's desk. A few moments later, Jimmy joined them.

I considered this Justice League of Perverts and I thought: "*That's* who would buy a gallon of lube."

This place sucks.

Day 144:

The break area TV has been locked onto the same channel for the past two months. And my break is timed to the broadcast and then re-broadcast of the same show.

If I have to watch Piers Morgan one more time, my descent into madness will be complete.

Day 145:

Someone wrote a joke on the V.O.A board tonight:

Q: How many Mikes does it take to change a light bulb?

A: None, because he's a dick.

I think he suspects I had something to do with it.

Day 146:

I always thought the most geographically-challenged person in the world was my sister, who once famously admitted she got the relative positions of North and South Dakota mixed-up. Which is *really* stupid when you think of it. Everyone knows South Dakota is bigger.

But then, last night. But then, Matt.

I got to work a few minutes early and sat down in the break area to watch a little SportsCenter. Soon Matt sits down and I brace myself for what is coming.

I only have to wait twenty seconds.

Seeing a score for the Xavier-Tennessee college basketball game, Matt offers the following:

"Xavier is my favorite New York City college."

The smart thing, of course, is to say nothing.

I think I may have already mentioned that I am not a smart man.

Me: "Do you realize your favorite New York City school is in Cincinnati?"

Matt: "Really?"

Me: "Yes, really."

Matt notices a score from the Appalachian State-Georgia game next and tries to save face.

Matt: "Appalachian State is in Pennsylvania. That one I know."

Me: "It's in Boone, North Carolina."

Matt: "Really?"

Me: "Yes. Really."

Matt: "I thought it was in Pennsylvania."

Me: "Only if Boone, North Carolina is in Pennsylvania."

He notes a score from the Texas Southern–Florida International game next.

Matt: "Texas Southern, I'm pretty sure, is in Texas."

"Pretty sure?" I think to myself.

"But it used to be called Texas Christian," Matt adds.

Me: "The school that used to be called Texas Christian is now called Texas Christian."

Matt: "Really?"

Me: "Yes. Really."

Matt is clearly getting frustrated and when he sees the score from the Kennesaw State–Michigan State game, he strikes.

Matt: "OK, Mr. Know-It-All, where is Kennesaw State?"

I sigh before responding, and then:

Me: "It's the state school of Kennesaw."

Matt (confused): "Where's Kennesaw?"

Me: "You know that pointy strip of land just above Michigan and connected to Wisconsin? That's Kennesaw."

Matt: "Wow, when did that happen?"

I stare at Matt in stunned silence for a moment, then reply "At the end of the Bush administration."

Matt ponders this for a moment.

Matt: "Cool."

Cool indeed, dumbass. Cool indeed.

Day 147:

About an hour into Sam's shift, his scanner sent him from the East to the West Mod. As he limped across the factory, The Sarge saw him and called out "Let's go, Jesse Owens, speed it up. I thought you people were supposed to be fast."

I am now haunted by what I saw in Sam's eyes.

I fear Mt. Samuel is about to erupt.

I'm not taking any chances. Instead of my bagged lunch, I'm going to Taco Bell.

Live Mas.

Live Mas indeed.

Day 148:

I turned once again, in vain, to the V.O.A., writing:

"Since you can force any associate to submit to a random drug test, can you also force Brad to submit to castration? It would make him significantly less creepy. Thanks."

Tonight, the response:

"We encourage all associates with personality conflicts to attempt to resolve them on their own before involving management."

I hear you loud and clear, V.O.A.

Tonight, in addition to my lunch and a sweatshirt, I've packed a ball gag, a bottle of chloroform, some rags, and a freshly sharpened emasculator.

Brad is going down.

Day 149:

I was inputting a missing item into my scanner when the kid with Tourette's entered my aisle.

Leaning over my shoulder, he conspiratorially whispered, "There's no need to scan every item; just wastes time. Just do one and hit complete. Scanner doesn't know how many items are actually in a bin, and as long as you're *positive* the item is not in there, no one will know you didn't scan them all."

"Thanks," I replied, before I caught it.

"I guess your Tourette's must come and go, huh?"

He looked down both aisles to be sure there was no one else around, then leaned back in.

"It's just an act."

"Really? So, you just thought it'd be a hoot to fake having a nervous system disorder?"

"Nah, man. It's not like that. Faking allows me to vent about this fucking place without getting into trouble.

Don't let on," he added, his finger placed up against the side of his nose, before moving on.

I was momentarily offended, but when I consider the constant fear that Sam will snap and go postal, or the race paranoia of Stovepipe Lincoln, using Abe as a talisman to ward off the threats of the white people, or Brad the sex-toy tester, I realize that this kid is a genius.

Perhaps the best way to protect oneself from the inmates of the asylum is to simply act like one of them. Like Stein says in Conrad's *Lord Jim*, "to the destructive element submit."

After nearly thirty weeks here, giving in and giving up has a lot of appeal. I'm not sure how much longer I can hold out.

I just want to go home.

Day 150:

The Inactive Gaylord that upset me so much last week has been replaced by one bearing a sign that read "Test Gaylord."

"OK, I'm game," I thought.

Going up to the Gaylord, I asked "Who won the National League batting title in 1998?"

No response.

Fair enough. Sports was not this Gaylord's best subject. I switched to history:

"In what year was the Battle of Waterloo fought, and who were the combatants?"

Again, no response.

Feeling slightly embarrassed for the Gaylord now, I decided to give it an easy one:

"What is 7 times 6?"

Nothing.

"Um, spell 'cat'?"

Again nothing.

I'm not sure this Gaylord is much better than the Inactive one.

Day 151:

Another annoying thing parents do to children is smugly chide them for honest mistakes. You make one oversight and suddenly they become Aesop, gleefully lecturing you on the weighty consequences of trivial issues.

Having long-since reached adulthood, I had assumed that I was now free and clear of this irritation.

But I was wrong. I work for The Company.

We are required to wear work gloves and use box cutters every shift; there are vending machines at each P.A. desk where these required items can be acquired.

But The Company limits the number you can get from the machines.

Me: "Why can't I get gloves from the vending machine?"

The Company: "Because you've reached the limit for this pay period."

Me: "There's a limit?"

The Company: "Yes. You can only get two pairs of gloves or two box cutters per pay period."

Me: "But I need gloves to work. It's a requirement. That *you* made."

The Company: "Well, what happened to your old gloves?"

Me: "The first pair ripped in two days, because the gloves you offer are pieces of shit."

The Company: "And the second pair?"

Me: "I forgot them at home because five days of twelve-hour shifts leaves me somewhat exhausted and not at my mental sharpest."

The Company (nodding smugly): "Well, then. Let this be a lesson to you."

I hate this place.

Day 152:

One of my friends asked me the following question on Facebook this morning:

"OK, Company expert, what do I do when I receive a totally wrong item? I got all the things I ordered, plus a total other package that has nothing to do with anything I ordered. Do I just ignore it? Do I let The Company know, and maybe somehow send it back? Please advise."

My response:

"I'd return it, unless it is something you like (because, hey, free present). But the reality is that what you hold in your hand is not an extra item that was mistakenly sent to you instead of someone else.

What you hold in your hand is someone's job.

When you send that package back and/or when the intended customer complains it did not arrive in time for Xmas, someone in the Pack and/or the Ship department is losing their job. The Company is not very forgiving about such mistakes. Zero tolerance. Sad, but true."

I think my friend thought I was joking.

Day 153:

Today Mike told me during stand-up that I was to go upstairs and wrangle totes. I assumed he selected me because he learned that I had spent ten years living in Texas and *not* because tote wrangling is widely-considered the worst job there is at the warehouse.

I dutifully went upstairs once the shift began, but returned to Mike's desk about five minutes later.

"I have no idea where the horses are kept," I informed him.

"What?"

"The horses. To wrangle the totes from."

"Oh. Very cute, Paul," he said in a tone that may have been condescending. "We don't use horses."

"So, we do it standing on the ground?"

"Yes, Paul, we do," in a tone that I am *sure* was condescending.

"Good," I said. "Because I left my chaps at home. Was nervous about chafing."

And back upstairs I went.

About ten minutes later, Mike came upstairs to find me walking around somewhat lost and confused.

"Paul," he shouted, "what the hell are you doing?"

"I cannot find the damn lassos anywhere!" I screamed in frustration.

"Jesus Christ, Paul! Just forget it. I'll get someone else to do it."

And just like that, my rodeo career was over.

This place sucks.

Day 154:

Matt again.

Matt: "Do you ever get tired?"

Me: "Is that a serious question?"

Matt: "I'm running a marathon next week."

The concept of this man, possessor of the most decidedly un-athletic body one could imagine, running a marathon, should have struck me as staggeringly absurd.

I should have laughed.

I should have mocked.

I should have jeered.

But absurdity is the very oxygen of this place, so I did none of these things.

I just accepted Matt's declared intention to waddle a marathon as just one piece of colored foil in the lunatic kaleidoscope that has become my world.

Me: "Wow. A marathon. That's impressive. How long have you been training?"

Matt: "I haven't started yet. I'm off tomorrow, so that's my plan. But I'm worried I'll be too tired. Sometimes on my off day, I fall asleep when I don't want to."

At this point, the smart thing to do would be to turn and run away.

But since I am most decidedly *not* a smart man, I responded.

Me: "I know what you mean. The other day I feel asleep in a dentist's chair."

Matt: "You went to the dentist?"

I blinked at Matt for a few seconds, mouth agape.

Me: "No. I have a dentist's chair in my living room."

Matt (clearly impressed): "That. Is. So. Cool!"

Me: "It's something."

After breaking away from Matt and resuming my pick path, I reflected that the first guy to run a marathon dropped dead afterwards.

That flicker of hope kept me going through the rest of my shift.

Day 155:

It occurs to me just how much my typical shift resembles Pac Man.

There is an established field through which I must successfully maneuver according to a pattern which I must discover through trial and error, while effectively avoiding a group of distinctive antagonists wandering the field intent on disrupting my progress.

Instead of Inky, Blinky, Pinky, and Clyde, I have Matt and his siren song of idiocy, Mike, arbitrarily invested with irrelevant power, Brad, potentially shooting ropes of jism in my path, and the Werther's lady, lustfully plying my innocence with offers of caramel delight.

The only thing missing is fruit.

There should be fruit.

Flickering, floating fruit.

That is the only way any of this make sense.

Day 156:

Tonight, an order of a Barbie doll, Dora the Explorer bubble bath, and a pair of laced crotchless panties.

I am so deeply, deeply disturbed by this.

Day 157:

I hold an advanced degree in English Literature. This means that I have been professionally trained to understand that our culture has produced some of the most profound explorations of the human condition; the brutal honesty of Cormac McCarthy, the sardonic judgment of T.C. Boyle, or the eloquent verses of Hank Jones.

Yet I spend my nights endlessly picking volume after volume of Bill O'Reilly.

Dante has *nothing* on this place.

Day 158:

A Day in the Life of a Company Picker

(A Play in One Act)

Scene: outside the single stall bathroom. Co-worker approaches door and tries to open it, only to discover it is locked.

He then knocks on the door.

Receiving no response, he stands in front of door for a few moments, then tries door handle again. He knocks on the door. Again.

Shortly after, the door opens and Paul exits, scowling.

PAUL: "C'm here! Let me show you something."

(Co-worker approaches Paul and door)

PAUL (pointing toward the bolt on the inside of the door): "You see this?"

CO-WORKER: "Um, yeah."

PAUL: "This is called a lock. When the door does not open, that means the door is locked. You following me so far?"

CO-WORKER: "Um, yeah."

PAUL: "Good. Now, when the door is locked *from the inside* — and since you've worked here longer than I have, I know you know this door locks from the inside — that means there is someone *inside* the bathroom. Still with me?"

CO-WORKER: "Um, yeah."

PAUL: "'Cause that's the only way the door gets locked, right?"

CO-WORKER: "Um, yeah."

PAUL: "Good. That being the case, there is *no fucking reason to knock after trying the handle*!!! Whoever is in there is busy, and they are not going to drop everything to let you in. Got that?"

CO-WORKER: "Um, yeah."

PAUL: "Now, if, after trying the handle, you find the door

locked, and you are standing *in front of* the door, there is *no reason* to try the handle *again* a few moments later. If you did not see anyone leave from your advantageous observation post *in front of the door*, that means that that person is *still in there*!!!! Understand???"

CO-WORKER: "Um, yeah."

As curtain falls, Co-worker enters bathroom, while Paul walks offstage, questioning every choice he has made in life.

Day 159:

As I scurried through section D on the 3rd floor, I saw Kevin in the high-end electronics cage.

"Kevin Koswalski, as I live and breathe, whatever are you doing in that cage?"

Without missing a beat, Kevin replied, "Paul, whatever are you doing in yours?"

Touché, Mr. Koswalski, *touché.*

Day 160:

I was late into a dismal, languid night in the West Mod, half-heartedly searching a bin for the Sexy Kitten Naked Lady with Inflatable Boobs Apron my scanner was insisting someone, somewhere wanted to own, when I first heard the sobs.

At first, I just assumed that it was my soul crying, since it was living in a world where one can buy a Sexy Kitten Naked Lady with Inflatable Boobs Apron.

As they continued, I realized the tears were coming from the next aisle over. Peeking around the corner, I saw Mabel, bent over her cart, weeping. Mike's nightly harassment had finally broken her. Tonight, Mike had given her a written warning because last week she came in at 99% of rate. And so, this sixty-three-year-old woman who had worked here for almost three years, somehow always making rate and doing her best to bring a small sliver of joy in the form of small balls of sugar and corn syrup on a stick to everyone she met, was one step away from unemployment. I thought this wrong and unfair, and told her so.

"It's all so fucking impertinent," was Mabel's cry in response.

I was, I must admit, knocked a bit off balance by this most grandmotherly of grandmothers rolling out the F-bomb, and in virtually any other situation I would have found her incongruous pairing of words delightfully hilarious. But my helplessness at her position killed any latent humor the moment may have had.

And that's when I felt it. The Homestretch Treat in my pocket.

Lately, my youngest son has been giving me candy that he knows I love from his Xmas stocking stash to help "get through your work day." Twizzlers one night, a roll of Sprees the next. The only caveat he insisted upon was that I could not get into them until after 3 a.m. (Hence, the Homestretch Treat). It was a kindness that truly touched me, and by giving me something to look forward to it did make the night somewhat more bearable. And tonight, I had a grand prize in my pocket; a cherry flavored Tootsie Roll lollipop, one of my favorite candies on the planet. As Mabel fought valiantly to hold back a new wave of tears, I began to finger the treat, and I knew what I had to do.

I pulled it out, closed Mabel's hand over it, leaned over and whispered in her ear "*illegitimi non carborundum.*"

Good advice for us all, I suppose. Good advice for us all.

Day 161:

Although it has failed me in the past (repeatedly), tonight I once again turned to the V.O.A. for help, writing:

"Have You Seen Me?"

Next to this question, I drew a humanoid outline, then added:

"Missing! Mike's Soul."

"If found, return to P.A. desk, West Mod."

"Generous Reward offered!"

Today's response:

"If you are missing an item, please visit the Lost and Found rather than tie up the V.O.A with such matters."

But there is no Lost and Found here.

I fear Mike's soul is lost for good.

I shall pray for him.

Day 162:

It was really just a matter of time.

I have succumbed to the bane of the Picker—plantar fasciitis, stemming from overwork during peak season.

Additionally, a tendon on the bottom of my foot is torn, only partially attached to my heel.

There are several days when I cannot walk after a shift and I'm forced to crawl around the house.

My children cry when they see this, and beg me each night not to go to work.

They fear I will never be able to run and play with them.

(I share this fear, although I keep that to myself.)

I asked my podiatrist what I can do to get better.

His response: "Get a different job."

He said he was willing to write me a prescription to that effect, which I thought was kind of him.

I'd rather have some Percocet, though.

Day 163:

I really did not want to head back to work tonight. In fact, I was ready and willing to volunteer for the catheter-insertion training at the local clinic instead before my wife talked me out of it.

And boy am I glad she did. Otherwise I would have missed out on the following conversation with Matt:

Matt: "Hey, be careful if you use the bathroom at the back of the East Mod. The lock is jammed or something."

Me: "Yeah, I know. On Tuesday I took a dump in there (in direct violation of corporate policy) and I couldn't for the life of me get the door to open."

Matt: "Did you ever get out?"

Day 164:

For me, being sent to the East Mod or the West Mod is of little concern, akin to choosing death by boredom or death by fatigue.

But for Brad, I realize, this is a question of some legitimate angst, for all the good porn is in the East Mod, but the majority of the sex toys are in the West.

So, this place has taught me empathy, and I am richer for it.

Day 165:

Today I filled an order consisting of a 16-lb. bag of cat food (retail price $12.78) and a 10-lb. bag of rabbit food ($9.00).

With a little outside-the-box thinking and the suppression of sentiment, this person could spend $0 on pet food next time around.

Day 166:

I stood at the intra-section aisle linking Sections G and H.

I looked left as far as I could see. The Sarge was patrolling the area around his HR section; Mike scowled from behind the P.A. desk; Stovepipe Lincoln flashed into view, chanting his skewed homage to the Great Emancipator, and there, at the furthest reaches of my eyesight, was the V.O.A. board, that white-space nothingness where ideas, opinions and concerns went to die.

I looked to my right. Brad lurked a few aisles back, suspiciously close to a bin; Matt passed into view moving from G to H; in between the two and stretching back to the end of the Mod, I saw dozens of pickers, representing a kaleidoscope of idiocy, mental fugue, and spiritless automation.

And I thought of Steelers Wheel.

In 1972, five Scottish would-be philosophers offered to the world the following statement on the condition of man:

"Clowns to the left of me, jokers to the right, here I am, stuck in the middle..."

It's like they knew my very soul.

Day 167:

Maybe if we all just decided that we're ok waiting a few days longer to receive our impulse buys, my children would not cry as they see me crawl through the house.

I suggested as much to my friends and family on Facebook and asked them to pledge not to renew or enroll for The Company's two-day-free-shipping rewards program.

No one has responded.

I think they think I'm joking.

Or maybe I just need new friends.

Day 168:

They have broken Sam.

I found him in the East Mod tonight fighting desperately to hold back tears. The pain in his feet has reached the point where he has to walk on the outside edges of them, and still each step sends jolts of pain up his legs.

"I can't keep doing this," he moaned. "I don't know how I'll get to the next aisle, let alone finish the night. They're going to can me."

Seeing this towering man once so full of vigorous rage reduced to such a state left me both scared and helpless.

Powerless to adequately address Sam's plight, I offered what assistance I could. Bearing as much of his weight as I could on my shoulders, I guided him over to a break area at the back of the Mod and told him to sit down.

Sam: "But they'll get me for T.O.T."

Me: "No, they won't. Give me your scanner. You just rest."

For the next fifteen minutes, I alternated picks and scanners.

106

It was paltry aid for certain, but I didn't know what else to do.

I truly hate this place.

Day 169:

Today Matt approached me (someone really needs to put a bell on this guy) resplendent in his Baltimore Ravens jersey. As if resuming an argument, he puffs out the "Ravens" emblem with both thumbs and declares, "Like I said, we got hosed today."

"Yeah," I responded, "it was a close game." (41-7).

I assumed my contribution to the discussion was over, but then he says, "No worries. My Ravens will make the playoffs next week and make another Super Bowl run."

"Um, Matt, they can't make the playoffs. They've been eliminated."

"I have faith."

"It has nothing to do with faith; it's math. They are two games behind Cincinnati with only one game left."

"I'm not worried."

"Matt, (I realize now that I'm shouting), they would have to win 2 out of the next 1 games! That is not mathematically possible."

Matt smiled, put a finger alongside his nose, and said, "Nothing is impossible."

Am I glad I smuggled that hip flask into work tonight.

Day 170:

I picked the film *Soylent Green* on DVD and it got me thinking:

The film and this place have a lot in common.

In the world of the film, the most wise and experienced members of society are sacrificed to sustain a culture that isn't worth sustaining.

Here, dozens of Pickers I've met hold M.B.As, M.As, and Ph.Ds. and our ranks are littered with college professors from a wide array of disciplines.

And each night, these highly educated individuals are tasked with picking Yodeling Pickles and Fun Fin hats.

I could limp around yelling "Soylent Green is people!" but I suspect no one would care.

A pox on this place

Day 171:

As I limped through the Mods, the pain in my feet intolerable, one of the Company trainers led a pod of new hires past my aisle. At the back of the group, beaming a grin at me, was Jason. He had served his 45-day time out and was back in the game. Before the group moved on to the next training station, he managed to whisper to me

"We found a new house we're saving for." Another grin and a thumbs up accompanied the news.

Nothing, not my feet, not Mike nor Matt, not even a goddamn yodeling pickle, could wipe the grin off of my face the rest of the shift.

I have no doubt Mike thinks I'm stoned. A random drug test surely looms in my near future.

Day 172:

I decided it was time again to try to make up with Mike. Knowing his drive for damaging out items, I brought to his desk a box of hair dye and said I thought it should be damaged out.

He did the required six-sided check, then said, "Paul, I don't see a problem."

"It's right here," I replied, pointing at the issue and beaming my best "I'm-a-good-worker" smile at him.

He tried again, and still was flummoxed. So I had to explain. "It says here on the box that this is semi-permanent hair coloring."

"Um, yeah?"

"Well, as I'm sure you know, 'permanent' means 'remaining unchanged indefinitely.' There aren't *degrees* of permanent. Permanent is permanent, so there can be no such state as 'semi-permanent.' Therefore, this product is logically as well as semantically damaged."

I gave him the smile again for good measure.

He rubbed his face with his hands (which I've noticed he does a lot) and said "Paul, just get back to work"

"Well, if that's your attitude, I'm not even going to mention the phone protective case."

"What about it?"

"It's cracked."

"Then damage it out!" he suggested tersely.

"But a cracked protective case seems more like an existential issue to me."

"For the love of God, please. Just *please* get back to work."

I glanced back as I turned the corner into the Mod and saw him face down on the desk with his hands folded over his head. He may have been crying.

I don't think he likes me very much.

Day 173:

When the fill-in P.A. — Mike has taken a few days leave-of-absence, "to clear his head" the story goes — noticed I was limping, he suggested I go to AssociateCare, the on-site medical center, to get some treatment.

"Good idea," I said. "I've been meaning to have a doctor look at my feet."

"There isn't a doctor at AssociateCare."

"Oh. The nurse, then."

"Ah, there isn't a nurse there either."

"Ok. Then who *is* there?"

"I don't know. Just some guy."

"Has this guy taken any classes, like First-Aid or CPR?"

"I don't think so."

"Does he have *any* training or relevant experience?

"Not that I know of."

"And why should I go there again?"

"Well, he can give you some aspirin."

"You think he can get the child-proof lid off?"

(After a moment's pause): "Yeah, I think he can."

Instead of going to AssociateCare for some aspirin, I limped back into the Mod, closed my eyes real tight and kept repeating: "This can't be real. None of this can be real."

I want to go home.

Day 174:

Mummenschanz on DVD!

The asteroid can *not* get here soon enough!

Day 175:

I wrote the following on the V.O.A.:

"I suggest that The Company institute a warehouse-wide minute of anguished screaming at the top of every hour.

It would help team morale to know that we are all suffering equally."

The response: "We will no longer accept comments from this user ID."

Day 176:

This past peak season, the warehouse set many records:

·highest daily volume of goods shipped.

·highest weekly volume of goods shipped.

·highest seasonal volume of goods shipped, beating the previous record by more than 500,000 items.

What did we tired workers get for a bonus for all of our hard work?

Most of us are receiving weeks of being sent home early without pay because The Company wants to artificially-create a reasonable backlog of items purchased. They don't want non-Rewards Program members to get their stuff too quickly, as Corporate fears that will de-value those memberships.

Having my shift cut short and losing out on the expected pay is an inconvenience for me, as this is a second-income job. But to many of my co-workers, for whom this is their primary or only source of income, this represents a significant hardship.

Not everyone got this reward for peak season efficiency, though.

Sam's reward was being fired.

The continual wear and tear of peak season resulted in plantar fasciitis and a doctor's note (from a member of The Company's approved health network) limiting him to light duty only.

Mike had him sweep the factory.

So instead of walking for ten continuous hours pushing a cart, Sam now had to walk ten continuous hours pushing a broom.

A few days later, Sam was fired because he could no longer perform the job for which he had been hired.

There was another co-worker (whom I did not know, but to whom I was introduced by the memorial placard placed in the break room) who also received a special bonus for his peak performance work.

His bonus was death.

An otherwise healthy (as far as anyone knew) male worker in his 40s, he complained of not feeling well one night near the end of the third week of sixty-hour shifts. He decided to go home early and take a penalty for unapproved time off.

That night he died of heart failure.

He was the fifth male worker in his 40s, the story goes, to die of heart failure in the previous four peak seasons. Of course, all of them may have had other factors which contributed to their deaths, but Occam's Razor seems to suggest a different explanation.

But The Company's Rewards program memberships is really great.

It's so wonderful getting stuff two days after impulse buying it.

Day 177:

There's a girl, Carla, who finds Matt's existence particularly offensive. Any conversation with her quickly descends into an anti-Matt polemic.

Tonight, in the midst of a typical rant, she asked me: "Why do you even talk to him?"

In all honesty, I never really thought about that before.

After a few moments' consideration, I answered:

Me: "I guess because I understand him."

Carla: "What's that supposed to mean?"

Me: "It means I get it. The reason Matt shamelessly bandwagons his sports teams, the reason he simply assumes everyone is interested in his stories, the reason he is so obnoxious is, I think, the same reason Mabel hands out lollipops and Stovepipe Lincoln chants the Gettysburg address and, come to think of it, why I harass Mike. It's a declaration of identity; a way to scream into the faceless machinery of this place 'I exist! I'm not just a number on a rate chart!'"

I don't think she bought it, but I think I'm on to something here. Most of the aberrant behavior here (with the exception of Brad — he's just a twisted fuck) could be a desperate assertion of self to a persistently-depersonalized world.

Depressing, yes.

And dysfunctional.

But not without its perverse beauty.

Rumor has it, Mike returns from his sabbatical tomorrow. I'm looking forward to it.

Day 178:

I present Mike with a DVD of *The Karate Kid* and inform him: "This needs to be damaged out."

Mike: "Why? What's wrong with it?"

Me: "Ralph Macchio's in it."

Day 179:

Today Matt asked me which Mod I preferred. I found this to be a question of profound existential absurdity.

It's like being asked which caliber bullet you'd like to be shot in the head with.

"Matt," I answered, "I am thoroughly ambivalent."

His eyes grow wide. Then:

"Like a frog?"

I hate this fucking place.

Day 180:

My last day in the belly of the beast.

A blizzard has relieved me from the pain and suffering that was life as a warehouse Picker.

I made the attempt to drive in to work yesterday, but found the secondary roads around my house impassable. Last week, under similar circumstances, The Company granted amnesty to everyone who did not make it to work due to unsafe driving conditions. I assumed they would do the same this time, so I drove back home.

When I showed up for work today, I was fired.

All that is left to do is clear out my personal belongings

from my locker, and to sign a document acknowledging that I understood that I was terminated and thus could not be re-hired for forty-five days.

After once again trying in vain to convince The Sarge that I was not Hispanic, I signed the form (as "The Colonel of Death") and found myself standing on the outside steps where I had once wished upon a shooting star. While I was weighing the granting of one wish versus my lack of an Xbox, Kevin approached.

Kevin: "Heard you were fired."

Me: "Yeah."

Kevin: "Me too. Blizzard conditions and all."

Me: "Can't say I'm too broken up about it."

Kevin: "Me neither."

Me: "So what are you going to do now?"

Kevin: "Guess I'll try to get my old job back. Doesn't seem so bad now."

I shook his hand and wished him well.

As he walked away, he turned and said: "I'm glad to see you got out of your cage, Paul. The world is before us; where to go?"

I knew exactly where I was going.

I was going home

II

Postscript

Day 1, Post-Firing:

I assumed that the sudden plunge back into unemployment would be frightening and anxious, but as I get ready for bed tonight — for the first time in months at a time when the rest of my family is also getting ready for bed — I find that tucking my sons into bed and kissing my wife good night leaves me, in fact, feeling *quite* fulfilled.

III

Post-postscript

Day 2, Post-Firing:

In *The Godfather, Part III*, Al Pacino famously laments, "Just when I thought I was out, they pull me back in."

I think I know how he feels.

Today I got a call from The Company's HR department, asking why I had not been showing up for work the last two days.

I hate that place.

IV

Post-post-postscript

VI

Post-post-postscript

Day 46, Post-Firing:

I guess my forty-five-day time out is over.

I received another call from HR, suggesting I re-apply for employment.

"We have," I was told, "many exciting positions for you."

I reflected for a moment, and asked for doggie-style.

"Um, excuse me?"

"You know, face down, ass up. That seems like the most appropriate position."

I further suggested the use of a ball gag.

"I see no reason," I explained, "why the anguished screams of my disintegrating soul should intrude upon the working environment of others."

The woman from HR did not reply.

I think she thought I was joking.

Acknowledgments

What you hold in your hands is the result of seven years of, as T.S. Eliot would say, "visions and revisions." The list of people who have contributed during this seven-year transformation is vast, and it is a certainty that I will be forgetting individuals who deserved not to be forgotten. To them, I ask forgiveness. Such an oversight is the result of a faulty memory, not intention.

I feel I must begin with a tip of the cap to all of my fellow sufferers (The Company euphemistically calls them "co-workers"). We struggled side-by-side, each and every night, and while I may not always have liked you (I'm looking at you, Matt) and may still not (you know who you are), you always had my empathy. And if you are still trapped there — although I can't imagine many of you are (maybe just The Sarge) — you still do.

From among the list of the fellow-damned, I would like to specifically thank Brian Mitchell and James Stezenko; your friendship, support, and commiseration were vital. I would not have been able to endure without.

And speaking of enduring, I must acknowledge the many contributions of Chris Juhasz, ranging from a pot of coffee and a hot-water foot bath waiting for me as I began to write after every shift, to her precise editing eye at every step along the way.

I would also like to thank Lila Guterman, the entire Kankel family, and Scott Rettberg. This project may never have progressed beyond pithy Facebook posts meant to entertain my friends, had not Lila mentioned that as part of the Kankel family's 2013 holiday season celebration, she gathered them round and read my posts to much laughter and fanfare; or had not Scott asked if I would accept a friend request from his wife, so she could read these same posts. Without this affirmation, I might not have had the motivation to push this project into another form.

And speaking of those other forms, I must thank Moumin Quazi and Marilyn Robitaille, editors of the *Langdon Review of the Arts in Texas,* who were gracious enough to publish an abridged version of this work in 2015; Carol Coffee Reposa, who was instrumental in getting *Fulfillment* serialized in the literary journal *Voices de la Luna* from 2017-18; and Ken Hada, who accepted an excerpt of the work for the 2018 Scissortail Literary Festival. Without the validation of their support, it is unlikely this project would have continued.

Special thanks to Roxie Kirk and everyone at Fine Dog Press for embracing this project with such enthusiasm and guidance.

I would also like to thank Kylie George and Kerry Cohen for their assistance, contributions, and support.

And finally, it is with profound gratitude and humility that I must thank Woodstok Farley and Hank Jones, who have been so unconditional in their love and support. It would be reductive to say that without your many and sundry contributions this book would not exist, for your impact falls well beyond just this book. To call you both "friends" is to simply acknowledge the limitation of language. I am blessed, lucky, and unworthy.

About the Author

Living what could be charitably called a nomadic life, Paul Juhasz was born in western New Jersey, grew up just outside of New Haven, Connecticut, and has spent appreciable chunks of life in the plains of central Illinois, in the upper hill country of Texas, and in the Lehigh Valley in Pennsylvania. Most recently seduced by the spirit of the red earth, he now lives in Oklahoma City. Believing visceral experience is the essential force behind imagination, he has worked at a warehouse fulfillment center, manned a junk truck, and driven for Uber, all to gather material and characters for his poetry, fiction, and creative non-fiction, a trait that has led a friend and fellow writer to label him "the blue-collar George Plimpton." His debut book, *Fulfillment: Dairy of a Warehouse Picker,* has been published by Fine Dog Press.

CPSIA information can be obtained
at www.ICGtesting.com
Printed in the USA
FSHW011257220720
72376FS

9 781733 979573